Anatomy
OF THE
Qur'an

G.J.O. Moshay

CHICK
PUBLICATIONS
Ontario, Calif 91761

For a complete list of distributors near you,
call (909) 987-0771, or visit
www.chick.com

Copyright ©2007 G.J.O. Moshay

Published by:
CHICK PUBLICATIONS
PO Box 3500, Ontario, Calif. 91761-1019 USA
Tel: (909) 987-0771
Fax: (909) 941-8128
Web: www.chick.com
Email: postmaster@chick.com

Printed in the United States of America

ISBN: 978-07589-0674-8

Preface

Islam is no longer a religion we can ignore in America or elsewhere in the Western world. It must be thoroughly studied by both Christians and Muslims. The best way to start is by examining the Muslim's 'bible,' the Qur'an.

The Qur'an has 114 chapters called 'suras.' Each chapter is numbered and given names such as: The Bee, The Spider, The Cow, Maryam, The Jinn, The Cave, Muhammad, Joseph, etc. This author uses chapter numbers rather than the names.

This book quotes several translations of the Qur'an. However, the primary two are: *Interpretation of the Meanings of the Noble Qur'an in the English Language,* by Dr. Muhammad Taq-ud-Din Al-Hilali and Dr. Muhammad Muhsin Khan, 1985; and *The Holy Qur'an: Text, Translation and Commentary* by Yusuf A. Ali (1938).

Sometimes, when looking for a reference in the Qur'an, you may need to check a few verses before or after the verse number cited. This is because verse numbers sometimes vary in some translations.

Also, various editions of English translations of the Qur'an translate words differently. For instance, the same Arabic word can be translated "apostle," "messenger," or "prophet." Sometimes, two different editions of the same translation interchange these and other words.

It is the hope of the author that this book will motivate Christians to share the love of Jesus with Muslims and inspire the Muslim reader to reconsider his ways.

Contents

Dedication

To all earnest seekers of truth
Especially
To all Muslim friends
Yearning for the truth
That leads to Heaven's route
and hope as Time ends.
And to the memory of my friend's mother
Deborah
who is now with the Lord.

1

The Miracle of The Qur'an

For an average Muslim, there is no dispute about the prodigy and matchlessness of the literary quality of the Qur'an. For him, that is the greatest evidence of the divine origin of the book. In the collection of Islamic tradition, *Mishkat'ul Masabih*, the editor wrote:

> "The Qur'an is the greatest wonder among the wonders of the world. It repeatedly challenged the people of the world to bring a chapter like it, but they failed and the challenge remains unanswered up to this day... This book is second to none in the world according to the unanimous decision of the learned men in points of diction, style, rhetoric, thoughts and soundness of laws and regulations to shape the destinies of mankind." [1]

---

[1] *Mishkat'ul Masabih* (Collected by Imam Hussain Al-Baghawi, with commentary by Al-Haj Maulana Fazlul Karim (Lahore: The Book House) Vol. 3, p. 664.

The Qur'an says of itself:

"And this Qur'an is not such as could ever be produced by other than Allah (Lord of the heavens and the earth), but it is a confirmation of (the revelation) which was before it [i.e. the *Taurât* (Torah), and the *Injil* (Gospel), etc.], and a full explanation of the Book... wherein there is no doubt from the Lord of the *Alamin* (mankind, jinns, and all that exists).

"Or do they say, 'He (Muhammad) has forged it'? Say: 'Bring then a *Sura* (chapter)[2] like unto it, and call upon whomsoever you can besides Allah, if you are truthful!'"[3]

Again we read:

"And this {the Qur'an} is a blessed Book which We have sent down, confirming (the revelations) which came before it..."[4]

Most of Muhammad's listeners were illiterate. But how does a modern historian or literary man react to these claims? *The Muslim Students Association* at the University of California says on their website:

"Prophet Muhammad (saas) was the final Messenger of Allah to humanity, and therefore the Qur'an is the last Message which Allah has sent to us. Its predecessors such as the Torah, Psalms,

---

[2] "Sura" or "Surah" refers to "Chapters" in the Qur'an.
[3] Sura 10:37-38 (Dr. Muhammad Taqi-ud-Din Al-Hilali and Dr. Muhammad Muhsin Khan, 1985).
[4] Surah 6:92 (Hilali).

and Gospels have all been superseded. *It is an obligation – and blessing – for all who hear of the Qur'an and Islam to investigate it and evaluate it for themselves.* Allah has guaranteed that He will protect the Qur'an from human tampering, and today's readers can find exact copies of it all over the world. The Qur'an of today is the same as the Qur'an revealed to Muhammad (saas)." *(Emphasis mine).*

Are Muslims ready for such an investigation and evaluation of the Qur'an? It is a challenge we must take up.

Proof of Prophet-hood

When Muhammad presented his mission to the Jews, he had said that he had been foretold in the Jewish scriptures.[5] The Jews demanded signs, miracles and an accurate foretelling of the future as proof of his claim of prophet-hood. When God told Israel, through Moses, that He would give them a special prophet like Moses, He told them how to recognize him, and how to identify a false prophet:

> "But the prophet, which shall presume to speak a word in my name, which I have not commanded him to speak, or that shall speak in the name of other gods, even that prophet shall die.
>
> "And if thou say in thine heart, How shall we know the word which the LORD hath not spoken?
>
> "When a prophet speaketh in the name of the LORD, if the thing follow not, nor come to pass,

---

5 Sura 61:6; 7:157

that is the thing which the LORD hath not spoken, but the prophet hath spoken it presumptuously: thou shall not be afraid of him."[6]

So the Jews had a reason to demand signs and accurate prophecies to authenticate Muhammad's claims. But Muhammad said he had no such power.

"So, how do we believe you?" they asked. "God has shown us how we can prove a claim of being 'the Prophet' foretold in Deuteronomy 18:18; prove yourself.'" Muhammad replied that his "sign" or "miracle" is the Qur'an itself (even though the Qur'an was not yet complete as a book at that time). Verses of the Qur'an are called *Ayat*, which means signs, evidences, verse, lessons, revelations, laws, etc).

What is the "miracle" or "clear sign" about the recitations (or the sheets containing his revelations)? He said the "clear sign" is that the Qur'an is so wonderful that no human beings, even if they joined hands together with spirits, would ever be able to produce such a sublime book.[7] It is in this regard that a South African based Islamic teacher, Ahmed Deedat, wrote a pamphlet, *Al-Qur'an, the Ultimate Miracle.* Deedat claims that he has proved 'mathematically' that the Qur'an descended from heaven, and is free from human instrumentality.

Now we have to examine the Qur'an to discover the miracle of its origin. Moreover, if the Qur'an is the major miracle Muhammad performed—the basic proof of

---

6 Deuteronomy 18:20-22
7 Sura 17:88; Sura 13:31; Sura 2:23

his prophet-hood—then the validity of Islam stands or falls on the authenticity of the book. That is why a sincere Muslim needs to be patient and examine analytically what is being presented here. Sentiment won't help us.

Many Muslim historians say that Muhammad was illiterate, an unlettered man. The argument is that if the man was not learned, and such a book came through him, it must have been a great miracle indeed. Qur'an translator and commentator, Abdullah Yusuf Ali, explaining this miracle, says Muhammad:

> "… had a most wonderful knowledge of the scriptures. This was a proof of his inspiration. It was a miracle of the highest kind, a "sign" which **everyone could test then, and everyone can test now.**" [8]

If Muhammad had a most wonderful knowledge of the scriptures, i.e. the Jewish and Christian scriptures, that means these scriptures existed at the time of Muhammad. However, this same Yusuf Ali contradicts himself later by saying the Jewish and Christian Scripture "was **lost** BEFORE Islam was preached."[9]

He had said that "everyone" could test the accuracy of the Qur'an **then,** i.e. at the time of Muhammad. The question is: How could everyone test the accuracy of Muhammad's knowledge of the scriptures if the standard scriptures against which such a test could be made were already **lost?**

---

[8] Ali, A. Yusuf, *The Holy Qur'an: Text, Translation and Commentary* (Beirut: Dar Al Arabia Publishing, 1938) Commentary No. 1132.
[9] Ali, A. Yusuf, *The Holy Qur'an: Text, Translation and Commentary,* Appendix II, p. 285.

Ali says, "everyone can test now (Muhammad's) perfect knowledge of the scriptures." If everyone can test Muhammad's knowledge (as shown in the Qur'an) **now**, why are many Muslims today vehemently opposed to a scrutiny of the Qur'an? Why do they regard critics of the Qur'an as enemies of Islam? Are they saying that anybody who really believes in Islam must not examine the Qur'an? They warn their followers not to read the Bible, except the quotes they extract to prove or disprove a claim.

In this book we shall test this knowledge of Muhammad, as displayed in the Qur'an, and call on every sincere lover of truth to relax and let us do the testing together.

If we can test Muhammad's knowledge, against what will we test? Of course, against the scriptures (that is, the Bible) that was in existence before he came.

But as we have hinted earlier, some Muslims who are afraid of such testing will say, "Oh, the Bible has been changed," or "The original Bible no longer exists." Such a claim is very cheap because it does not encourage scholarship. If the book the Qur'an came to confirm had been changed or is lost, against what then are we going to test the accuracy of the Qur'an? Allah tells Muhammad:

> "But why do they {the Jews} come to thee {Muhammad} for decision, while they have Taurât (Torah) in which is the plain Decision of Allah?…"[10]

Sura 5:47-48, 66, 68 says:

> "Let the People of the *Injeel* (Gospel) judge by

---

[10] Sura 5:43 Yusuf Ali

what Allah has revealed therein. And whosoever does not judge by what Allah has revealed (then), such (people) are the *Fasiqun* [the rebellious i.e. disobedient (of a lesser degree)] to Allah.

"And We have sent down to you (O Muhammad) the Book (this Qur'an) in truth, confirming the Scripture that came before it, and a witness guarding it in safety: so judge among them by what Allah hath revealed, and follow not their vain desires, diverging from the Truth that hath come to thee... If only they {Jews and Christians} had stood fast by the Law, the Gospel, and all the revelation that was sent to them from their Lord, they would have enjoyed happiness from every side...

Say, O people of the Scripture (Jews and Christians)! You have nothing (for guidance) till you act according to the Taurât (Torah) the Injeel (Gospel), and what has been sent down to you from your Lord..."

From the above, some things are clear:

1. The Law (the first part of the Bible), and the gospel were both available at the time of Muhammad, and were in the hands of the Jews and Christians.

2. These books were sent by God.

3. They were authentic as the standard book against which the Qur'an has to be judged.

The Muslim Dilemma

To repudiate the Bible is to repudiate the Qur'an and the prophet-hood of Muhammad because Muhammad said the Bible is the Word of God. Yet to accept the Bible as the Word of God is to destroy the Qur'an because the Qur'an contradicts the Bible in many areas. The modern option is to try to prove that the present Bible is not the book Muhammad was referring to in the Qur'an.

Christians say it is this same Holy Bible we have today and ask, where is this book that the Qur'an refers to?

A Muslim wrote me and asked: "Who says we should use the Bible as a standard to judge the Qur'an?" My answer was that Allah says that Muslims and Christians should all use the Bible as the standard to judge the authenticity of the revelations of Muhammad.

Some Indisputable Historical Facts

1. Christians and Jews were in Arabia at the time of Muhammad.

2. Muhammad had much contact with them.

3. They had their Book with them at that time.[11]

4. Muhammad addressed them as "People of the Book" or "People of the Scriptures." This means the people who have the scriptures (as opposed to Arabs who depended on tribal religions based on oral tales).

5. Allah says:

> "And if thou (Muhammad) art in doubt concerning that which We {Allah} reveal unto thee, then

---

[11] Sura 2:4, 3:20, 75, Sura 4:136; Sura 5:47. 10:94

question those who read the Scriptures (that was) before thee."[12]

Another translation says, "...*ask those who possess the Message.*" Al-Hilali's translation says:

"...ask those who are reading the Book [the Taurât (Torah) and the Injeel (Gospel)] before you..."

Muslims are confused about who is being addressed in this Sura 10:94. Some say it is Muhammad. Some say it is those who were listening to Muhammad. Qur'an translator, Muhammad Pickthall says it is Muhammad. Al-Hilali and Muhsin Kahn also believe it is Muhammad.

Regardless, the instruction is the same, and goes in essence: If you Arabs are in doubt about the revelations of Muhammad, consult the Christians and Jews who have the original revelation. Since this is the case, the Bible could not have been lost or corrupted at that time.

6. The sixth indisputable fact is that Allah tells Muhammad:

"And We sent not (as Our Messengers) before you (O Muhammad) any but men whom We sent revelation... So ask of those who know the Scripture... if you know not."[13]

Here, Allah was aware that Muhammad did not know everything. What then was Allah's advice to Muhammad? "Go and learn from those who know the Bible."

But today, when a sincere Muslim is confused, he goes

---

[12] Sura 10:94 (Pickthal)

[13] Sura 16:43 (Al Hilali et al). The author ignores the interpolations of the editors which are not part of the Qur'anic text).

to his Imam or so-called "Islamic scholar." The Imam presents a distortion of the truth and the Muslim inquirer gets more confused. Even in this verse and in many verses, the translators, Al-Hilali and Muhsin Khan, have inserted many statements that are not part of the Qur'anic text to make the Qur'an say what they want it to say!

The Bible in the Qur'an

Sheikh Ahmed Deedat, "the great Islamic scholar of comparative religion" wrote:

> "The Tawraat we Muslims BELIEVE in is not the 'Torah' of the Jews and the Christians... We... BELIEVE that whatever the Holy Prophet Moses... preached to this people, was the revelation from God Almighty, but Moses was not the author of those 'books' attributed to him by the Jews and the Christians. Likewise, we BELIEVE that the present Psalms associated with (David's) name are not that revelation (the Qur'an talks about)... We SINCERELY BELIEVE..." (Emphases mine).[14]

We have seen Allah in some earlier Qur'anic verses commanding Muslims to believe in all the scriptures that came before the Qur'an. But what is the response of the modern Muslim scholar?:

> "Yes, we believe in all these scriptures of the Jews and Christians; but they are lost; they no longer exist."

So how can you believe in what is non-existent, what

---

[14] Deedat, *Is the Bible God's Word?* (Durban, South Africa: Islamic Propagation Center, 1980) p 5.

you have never read? If you would not obey what those verses command you to do, then they are no longer valid and may as well be expunged from the Qur'an.

The best way to test the Qur'an, therefore, is to compare and contrast it with the Bible. In fact, there are many stories in the Qur'an that one cannot understand without referring to the Bible. Such stories have no context outside the Bible. Again the Qur'an says:

> "Say: 'O People of the Book! {Christians and Jews} ye have no ground to stand upon unless ye stand fast by the Law, the Gospel, and all the revelation that has come to you from your Lord.'"[15]

Here, the Qur'an says the Jews and Christians have no authority outside the scriptures that came through them. Allah does not say they should depend on the Qur'an or use the Qur'an as a standard of moral life and judgment. In any case, the Qur'an, as we know it today, was not compiled at the time Muhammad was speaking. It was several years after his death that a compilation started.

Yes, Muhammad enjoins us to refer to the Bible to verify his claims. We shall do just that, but first we want to examine the Qur'an on its own merits—the internal evidence of the divine authorship of the book.

> "And this is a Book {Qur'an} which We {Allah} have sent down, bringing blessings, and confirming (the revelations) which came before it..."[16]

---

[15] Sura 5:68 (Yusuf Ali)
[16] Sura 6:92 (Yusuf Ali); See also Sura 3:3

2

It Matters What You Believe

"...for he cometh, for he cometh to judge the earth: he shall judge the world with righteousness, and the people with his truth."[1]

THE God Almighty, Creator of the heavens and the earth, is not bound by tradition or any speculation by man. He has His truth and He will judge everyone by His truth. His truth is not variable.

The question is then, what is His truth? Where can we read this truth about God, the truth about man, the truth about the problem of man, the truth about the salvation of man? Is it in the Bible? Is the Bible the truth?

The Christian believes that eternal truth is not a book *per se*; it is a Person. This Person said:

---

[1] Psalm 96:13

"I am the way, the truth, and the life..."[2]

For a Christian, therefore, it is what a book says about that Person which determines whether or not it contains the truth. We believe the Bible to be the truth about the Truth. And that all truth in it points to the Truth.

However, what about the Qur'an, the sacred book of Muslims? Is it the truth? Is it the truth about the Truth or a lie about the Truth? Or is it a mixture of truth and lies? How do we assess the Qur'an in relation to the Bible? Are the two books the same? Since God will judge man with His truth, it follows that what a man believes about this will determine what judgment he will face. It is because of this that we will examine these questions.

First, let us ask ourselves: What claims does the Qur'an make of itself? We saw some in the previous chapter. But what are the literary and historical realities of such claims? What does the Bible say about the Qur'an? What does the Qur'an say about the Bible? How do typical Muslims today see the Bible? How do they compare it with the Qur'an?

On the question: What does the Bible say about the Qur'an, the answer is: NOTHING. But the Qur'an says much about the Bible. It says the Bible is the Word of God. It says the Qur'an has come to **confirm** what is in the Christian and Jewish scriptures (*Torah* or *Tawrat*, *Zabbur* and the *Injil*, which are now in one volume called the Old Testament and New Testament).[3]

---

2 John 14:6
3 Sura 5:46-48 (Al-Hilali)

At least 131 passages in the Qur'an refer to the Law, the Psalms and the Gospel. The Qur'an says that its own truth and validity must be verified against Biblical records, and that those who reject or sneer at these books of the Bible will be severely punished in hell fire by God.[4]

Because of pride, however, many Muslim writers today judge the Bible by what the Qur'an says. But that is not what the Qur'an says they should do. It says the Qur'an is to be judged by what the Bible says.

Again, Allah is quoted in the Qur'an as telling Muhammad:

> "Say: 'I am no bringer of new-fangled doctrine
> among the apostles, nor do I know what will be
> done with me or with you. I follow but that which
> is revealed to me by inspiration; I am but a Warner
> open and clear.'"[5]

He said he did not come with a new-fangled doctrine different from what the Apostles of the Bible brought. But how do we verify that? By crosschecking the doctrines of the Qur'an with what is taught by the old prophets and saints in the Bible. That is the ONLY solution. Muhammad does not say here that we should follow him sheepishly and he does not say (as many Muslims say today), that the Bible has been changed. He says, "Go and crosscheck." A Muslim who says he cannot crosscheck with the Bible must know he has no standard by which to judge the Qur'an. And that means he cannot be sure

---

[4] Sura 138, 4:136
[5] Sura 46:9 (Ali)

whether or not he has long been feeding on lies. Muhammad continues:

> "...nor do I know what will be done with me or with you (my followers). I follow but that which is revealed to me by inspiration."

The Hadith records:

> "The Prophet said, 'By Allah, though I am the Apostle of Allah, yet I do not know what Allah will do to me.'"[6]

We must realize this issue is beyond an unbendable religious sentiment. If the man we are following says he doesn't know his own fate in eternity or that of his followers, what are we to do? Do we say, "Okay, Brother Prophet, we will follow you all the same. We were born in this religion, so we must remain in it." Such a mindset would be stupidity. Muhammad himself does not say we should follow him like that. He says in essence: "verify my claims; study what I present as revelations and weigh them against the scriptures that existed before I was born. If you find disparities, you must choose which way to go."

It is unfortunate that many Muslims today (even those who are learned and are supposed to be investigative in their approach to life) prefer to swallow all the claims in the Qur'an without any thorough investigation—just because they were born into an Islamic family or because they fear persecution.

Because of the titles, popularity and maybe some mate-

---

[6] Dr. Kahn, Muhsin Muhammad, *The Translation of the Meaning of Sahih Al-Bukhari* (Lahore: Kazi Publications, 1979) Vol. 5, #266.

rial benefits they have in the religion, some of them see it as their duty to defend the Qur'an at the cost of reason and historical realities. They will, of course, have themselves to blame. If we find out at the end of our journey in life that we had all our life been deceived by some "fangled-doctrine" of a religion, whom shall we blame? Certainly not God, and not Muhammad. We already had the caution sign from Muhammad himself to find out about the Qur'an before believing it.

How do we find out? First, we begin to analyze the book sura by sura, and find out if there is any definite, sure, and satisfactory plan of salvation there. What if we are in doubt as to whether or not some of the things in the Qur'an are in the scriptures that came before it? What should we do? Listen to Allah again:

> "And if thou art in doubt concerning that which We (Allah) have revealed unto thee, then ASK those who have read the Scripture (or the Book, i.e. the Bible) before thee…"[7]

That is the solution. But today, very few Muslims ask. Even those who ask do not go to the right people. Rather, they go to their Imams, who use their Hadith (Tradition) to explain the Qur'an. Or sometimes, they use the Qur'an to explain itself. But that is not what the Qur'an says they should do. It says to ask the Jews and Christians because they have the Scriptures.

---

[7] Sura 10:94

Did the Qur'an Come to Replace the Bible... or as a Superior Book to the Bible?

The Qur'an verses we have examined clearly answer these questions. But many Muslim writers who should lead others to the truth think up reasons to reject the Bible and discourage their people from reading it. They discredit the Bible instead of coming to the book with humility to discover the truth of God's revelation to man. To this end these Muslims have written several books to ridicule the Holy Bible.

A Muslim, A.S.K. Joomal of South Africa, wrote a book he titled *The Bible: Word of God or Word of Man?* He concludes emphatically that the Bible is **not** the Word of God. Writing almost the same thing as Joomal, Ahmed Deedat, also from South Africa, wrote *Is the Bible God's Word?*[8]

Of course, Joomal and Deedat only echo what other Muslims and ungodly Western critics have written about the Bible. (Much of what some of them write, especially against the deity of Jesus, is from the Watchtower literature ("Jehovah's Witnesses"). Ahmed Deedat goes as far as saying that the Bible is a pornographic book. Christians will not throw up dust or become violent because of such invective Islamic publications. In fact, we are thankful for such books because they help us understand the Muslims' mind about our holy book. Consequently, it helps us to know their problem and how to help them.

---

[8] Deedat, Ahmed, *Is the Bible God's Word?* Lawyer John Gilchrist wrote a rejoinder to Deedat's book, called *The Qur'an and the Bible Series*. It can be downloaded at www.answering-islam.org/Gilchrist.

The average Muslim who has read the works of these writers does not regard the Bible as the Word of God. The day such a person accepts the Bible as the Word of God, he ceases to be a Muslim. By necessary implication, he must reject the Qur'an as the Word of God. This may not be easy. But we need to realize that it is what we believe that determines what we are in the presence of God, and what we shall be when we die. Because of this, it is incumbent upon us to study the Qur'an more seriously than ever. Whatever discovery we make will be for our own good. In Christianity, God does not compel us to believe anything. He wants us to use not only our faith but also our reason. This should also be applicable to Islam.

Appeal to Reason

In the Bible, God said, "Come now, and let us reason together…"[9] If anything makes a man violently opposed to thoroughly examining what he believes, it must be a demon and not the God who spoke the verse above. This applies to anyone—whether he calls himself a Christian or a Muslim.

God certainly expects us to use our sense of logic and reason to come to any conclusion in whatever we believe.

That is why He will hold everyone responsible for whatever he chooses to believe in on earth. God does not want man to believe just anything. His Word says, "Let no man deceive you with vain words…"[10] The Apostle Paul also says, "Prove all things; hold fast that which is good."[11]

---

[9] Isaiah 1:18
[10] Ephesians 5:6
[11] 1 Thessalonians 5:21

That is the attitude God wants us to have in our approach to the study of the Qur'an or any book that makes a claim of divine authorship; any book that attempts to possess our souls. And if leaders of a religion threaten those who want to do critical examination of its book, they give us the suspicion that the religion might be a deception.

It is therefore necessary for the Muslim to be patient and critically consider our examination of the Qur'an. We do not expect a Muslim to simply reject the Qur'an without much thought and critical evaluation. We know there are many people who prefer to live in ignorance. They are offended by anything that calls for a more critical re-examination of whatever they have believed for a long time.

This book is simply an appeal to the mind and heart of intelligent Muslims to examine the facts, then draw their own conclusions. We cannot claim to be intelligent and broad-minded and still hate scientific investigations of our beliefs.

This book is therefore not meant for all Muslims. It is only for those whose minds are not so small that they cannot accommodate what other people have to say about their beliefs. It is not meant for those who are afraid to think, or for those who think they cannot be wrong.

Approach to the Qur'an

Even though Christians and Muslims believe their sacred book is the Word of God, the nature of such belief is different. Christians believe the Bible was inspired by God. The Bible says that holy men of God wrote the words of the Bible as they were inspired by the Holy Spirit of God.[12] Some of the writings are historical narratives, some poetry, and some prophecy. Each book of the Bible bears the name of the person God used for the writing or the person in whose honor it was written (where such identification is necessary).

Muslims, on the other hand, believe the Qur'an descended from heaven and was given to Muhammad as a book, chapter by chapter on different occasions. Then the suras (chapters) were compiled together as a whole, and it has never changed since its "descent" from heaven. The message, style, language and structure are all heavenly. Or as some believe, the book had been in heaven, and Angel Jubril (Gabriel) only came periodically to dictate from it to Muhammad, who had it written down.

For Muslims, therefore, all the words in the Qur'an came from heaven. They are the very words of Allah, not the words of Muhammad or a historian. The Qur'an was already a book written and preserved in heaven before descent (Sura 43:4 Hilali). Muhammad simply received the suras and recited them to his audience. Devoted Muslims, therefore, revere the book as uncreated, and if ever created, it was made in heaven, and therefore is highly authentic on any issue it deals with.

When a Muslim sees in the Bible "The Gospel According to Matthew," he sneers and says, "How can this be the Word of God? These are the words of Matthew, Mark, Luke, John, and Paul. This is not the *Injil* (the gospel)

---

2 12 Peter 1:21

that God gave Jesus. Jesus was given a book called the *Injil*; where is this book? Instead of one gospel, you people now have **four different gospels** written by mere human beings."

In the Old Testament, Muslims see names like Moses, Joshua, David, Habakkuk, etc., and protest, "These are books written by human beings. This is not the *Tawraat* and the *Zabbur* that God gave as prepared books from heaven." The Muslim's belief about the Bible is taught in the Qur'an. Sura 57:27 says, "...and We (Allah) gave him (Jesus) the gospel."

This is an unfortunate misconception which has been passed on to Muhammad's followers over the ages. Jesus Christ was not given the gospel as a book. He brought the gospel, which means "Good News." But the gospel is NOT a book. It's a message delivered verbally and demonstrated practically. It is summed up in chapter 3 of John's gospel:

14 "And as Moses lifted up the serpent in the wilderness, even so must the Son of man be lifted up:

15 "That whosoever believeth in him should not perish, but have eternal life.

16 "For God so loved the world, that he gave his only begotten Son, that whosoever believeth in him should not perish, but have everlasting life.

17 "For God sent not his Son into the world to condemn the world; but that the world through him might be saved.

18 "He that believeth on him is not condemned:
but he that believeth not is condemned already,
because he hath not believed in the name of the
only begotten Son of God.

19 "And this is the condemnation, that light is
come into the world, and men loved darkness
rather than light, because their deeds were evil...

36 "He that believeth on the Son hath everlasting
life: and he that believeth not the Son shall not see
life; but the wrath of God abideth on him."[13]

This is what Jesus Christ preached to a religious leader
called Nicodemus. Even though man's sin makes him
an object of God's wrath and destined for hell, he does
not have to go to hell because God made a provision of
atonement and redemption through faith in His Son. He
preached this and called followers to go to cities and vil-
lages and proclaim this message. He did not give them a
book to deliver to people or recite from.

When Jesus died, these early disciples wrote down the
summary of His message and the story of His life. Christians do not have *four gospels!* It is the gospel (the Good
News of salvation) verbally presented, which was documented. Each writer focused on certain aspects of Christ's
life, His teachings and works. The Apostle John wrote:

"That which was from the beginning, which we
have heard, which we have seen with our eyes,
which we have looked upon, and our hands have
handled, of the Word of life; (For the life was

---

13 John 36 ,19-3:14

manifested, and we have seen it, and bear witness, and shew unto you that eternal life, which was with the Father, and was manifested unto us.)"[14]

So the gospel is not a book but a message. Yet it is not just a message. It is life. Jesus Himself is the message and the life of the message. He is the living Word of God; that is, the Word of God in a living form. What God gave mankind is not a book or books but a person. The written Word contains all we need to know about the living Word, the Person.

Christians believe the Bible is so precious that we must study it daily and meditate on it anytime, anywhere. To us, it is spiritual food. We encourage friends to read it, and sometimes give out free copies.

For Muslims, however, the Qur'an is so sacred that "only the pure should touch" it.[15] Apart from pagans, Christians are also not "pure" by the Islamic definition and standard because they worship Jesus Christ as the Son of God, instead of worshipping Allah, who has no son. Only pure Muslims and angels must touch the book.

A Christian is therefore an infidel or "misbeliever" to Muslims. Therefore, Muslims believe that Christians must not touch the Qur'an, much less read it. That is why many Muslims are highly enraged seeing the Qur'an quoted by non-Muslims. They believe the book would be desecrated by the infidel's touch. We see such an attitude as uncivilized and unreasonable.

---

[14] 1 John 1:1-2
[15] Sura 79-56:77

The first problem is if "only the pure" should touch the Qur'an, for whom is the book meant? If the Qur'an contains the way of salvation for the sinner, the impure, how then does he get saved if he is forbidden to touch the book? How will he read it if he wants to be saved?

As for the Bible, it is not too holy to be touched and read by a sinner. It is, in fact, meant for the sinner. It is a mirror. In it, the sinner sees how sinful he really is. He sees the judgment of God for his sins but he also sees the provision God has made concerning his sins, and how he can obtain God's mercy. Reading the Bible keeps the impure from sinning. It keeps him from further impurity. The more the impure reads it, the holier he becomes. Most people do not want to read the Bible because it talks of their dear sins and warns them to repent, which they don't want to hear. King David wrote:

> "Wherewithal shall a young man cleanse his way? by taking heed thereto according to thy word... Thy word have I hidden in mine heart, that I might not sin against thee... Thy word is a lamp unto my feet, and a light unto my path..."[16]

The Bible is first meant for the unclean, so he can study it and be clean thereby. To remain pure, he should read it daily.

Most Muslims do not know their Qur'an at all because they do not read it – because only "the pure" should touch it. So they content themselves with their normal prayers and recitation of the common verses that form part of

---

[16] Psalm 119:9, 11, 105

their daily liturgy, and a few verses the Imam repeats in his sermons.

Moreover, anyone who wants to touch the Qur'an must perform the *wud'u* ritual (ablution). So, to read it anytime one wants is out of the question. It is unlike a Christian who can go everywhere with a small Bible, which he or she can read anywhere. A Muslim is satisfied with chanting *La illaha il allah, La illaha il allah* on his prayer beads, sometimes for hours. Many of those who do read the Qur'an delight themselves in memorizing it or using it for charms. Portions are used as mascots; sometimes certain portions are copied with special ink on a board and washed with water and drunk.

Many who study the Qur'an are interested only in memorizing the few verses necessary to attack Christianity. We do not deny some serious scholarship by very few Muslims, but most make no attempt to study the book.

Many Muslims who study the Qur'an have been prompted by the challenges of Western scholars. Some Western scholars know the Qur'an more than most Muslims. A Muslim, especially, in Islamic countries, risks being condemned to death if he dares do any critical work on the Qur'an. When some see a questionable part, they gloss over it and pretend nothing is wrong.

Our intention in this project is not to make Muslims throw away their Qur'an, but to challenge them to study it and verify its claims. God does not want us to believe with our heart only. We must use our minds as well. We often flare up when someone goes deep to analyze our illogical beliefs and possible lies we believe. This happens when we use only our hearts, and not our minds. If people really used their minds as God expected them to regarding their religion, most deceived people would discover they have been building on sinking sand.

As we saw earlier, God calls every sinner to the Bible, and says:

> Come now, and let us reason together, saith the LORD: though your sins be as scarlet, they shall be as white as snow; though they be red like crimson, they shall be as wool."[17]

If God calls me to reason with Him on the sin question, I have the right to ask questions. But if a Muslim asks questions, his Imam might suspect him of having apostatized.

After reading a book, a Muslim asked his Imam questions about their religion. The Imam became very hostile and started persecuting him, suspecting that the young man might have come in contact with some "dangerous" Christians. The Imam is not being unfair. He is only following the Qur'an, which says readers should not question any "hidden meanings."[18] In Islam, it is the policy of "Ta abbudi" - the Qur'an must "be accepted without criticism."[19] In Sura 3:7 Allah says the Qur'an is clear enough for anyone to understand, but it quickly adds:

"But those in whose hearts is perversity follow the

---

[17] Isaiah 1:18
[18] Sura 3:5
[19] Gibb, H.A.R. and Kramers, *Dictionary of Islam*, p. 525.

part thereof that is not entirely clear, seeking discord, and searching for its interpretation, but no
one knows its true meaning except Allah."

A Muslim who asks probing questions about the Qur'an
is seen as having perversity in the heart and seeking discord. In the Hadith, Muhammad said:

**"Allah has hated you... for asking too many
questions."**[20]

Again in the Qur'an:

**"O ye who believe (Muslims). Ask not questions
about things which if made plain to you, may
cause you trouble."**[21]

This is a strong warning from Allah or Muhammad to
all Muslims. It says there are some things you will discover in the Qur'an that if you discover their meaning, you
would ask why you should remain in this religion. If you
go to your Imam, he too will not make such things plain
to you because he knows you will put a big question mark
on your continued stay in the religion. Several questions
will arise in your mind. However, Jesus says:

"And ye shall know the truth, and the truth shall
make you free."[22]

The truth frees a man from any form of bondage.

There are some facts about the history and origin of the
Qur'an, which if the truth is made plain, may cause an in-
quiring Muslim trouble. But a serious Muslim should be

---

[20] Dr. Khan, *Sahih Al-Bukhari*, Vol. 2, #555; Vol. 3, #591.
[21] Sura 5:101 (al Hilali)
22) John 8:32

ready for such trouble if he wants the truth. Truth is not found in the streets; it needs to be sought if anyone wants to be free. In the next chapter, we shall examine the origin of the Qur'an briefly.

Since our belief determines our life now before God and our fate in the future, we insist that before we can accept anything as golden and unassailable truth, it must submit itself to the crucible and pass the test of scientific examination. That is why a Muslim reader must see this book as very important and study it to the end.

3

Is There an Original Qur'an?

Many Muslims believe the original copy of the Qur'an which Allah gave to Muhammad still exists, and has been in circulation since the time of the prophet. This, they say, is unlike Christianity, where the "original" Bible is lost.

However, there never was an original copy of the Qur'an as a book. According to the Hadith, *Mishkat'ul Masabih*, the Qur'an was originally written in pieces and fragments on palm leaves, camels' ribs and shoulder blades, etc. *The Concise Encyclopedia of Islam* confirms that most of it was "preserved" in the memories of the reciters:

> "The Koran was collected from the chance surface on which it had been inscribed: 'from pieces of papyrus, flat stones, palm leaves, shoulder blades and ribs of animals, pieces of leather, wooden boards, and the hearts of men'"[1]

---

[1] *The Concise Encyclopedia of Islam*, p. 230.

Maududi also agrees that the "original" Qur'an was "on the leaves of date-palms, barks of trees, bones, etc" [2]

For those who believe the book descended from heaven we ask: did it descend in such fragments and on palm branches and those camels' shoulder blades? Are there no better things on which to preserve sacred documents in such a heaven?

Some other Muslims say, "No, the book did not descend in that manner. It was dictated to Muhammad piece-meal, and he had them copied on those materials."

That means if there is an original Qur'an, it must be these palm branches and leaves, camel shoulder blades on which the words in the Qur'an were *first* recorded, as well as the heads of the earliest reciters. Those were the original copies. Since Muslim leaders have not preserved this "original Qur'an", they must admit that the original Qur'an does NOT exist. If they can accept this humbly, the issue may not require further examination.

It is necessary to point out the fact that there was no compilation of these bits of records until about thirty years after the death of Muhammad. Moreover, many of the best reciters of the Qur'an in whose "breasts" (memory) many portions of the Qur'an were preserved were slaughtered during the Jihads that followed the death of Muhammad, especially, at the battle of Al Yemama. In other words, the heads that contained much of the Qur'an were lost in battle, and so their contents irretrievably lost!

_____

[2] Maududi, Abdullah, *The Meaning of the Qur'an* (Lahore: Islamic Publications Ltd., 1967) p. 17.

We must bear in mind that the Qur'an was not originally meant to be a written document, but verbal recitation. That is why it is called "Qur'an," from an Arabic word which means "recitation." That is why much of the Qur'an was based on what people recalled from what Muhammad recited. And since many of the best reciters were killed in battle, several versions, verbal and written, became prevalent in the Islamic communities after the death of the founder.

During his time, Muhammad himself mentioned four people whose memory of the Qur'an he said he trusted more than others among his followers. These include Abdullah ibn Mas'ud, Salim, Mu'dh (or Mu'az) bin Jabal, and Ubai (or Ubayy) bin Ka'b. All traditions agree that ibn Mas'ud was the most competent as he was always mentioned first by Muhammad.[3] Umar, one of the leaders of Islam, had feared that the whole thing being regarded as the Qur'an might be completely lost because of the death of the people who could recite much of it. He advised Abu Bakr, who was then the Khalif, to order the compilation. The text of ibn Mas'ud, which should be most reliable, was ignored during this compilation. When Umar became Khalif, he continued the project. When he finished, he kept it with Hafsah his daughter who was also a wife of Muhammad.

Several differences existed in this new text compared with the ones with the people mentioned above. Arthur Jeffery cites several examples of these differences, and an

---

[3] *Sahih Muslim,* Book 31, #6016-6029.

interested student can verify this in his book.[4] So, no one could be sure that the pieces collected were complete or authentic.

On the authority of Anas ibn Maalik, many sects developed because of these various versions. The disagreement led to a series of fights to defend the different versions. It was because of this that Uthman, who succeeded Umar, gathered all the records he could, using his own discretion to determine which sayings should be accepted and which to reject and edit. He formed a four-man editorial board headed by Zaid Ibn Thabith to edit the Qur'an and come out with one copy. Uthman made sure that he collected and destroyed all the other manuscripts that others had compiled and were reciting in Syria, Iraq and Armenia:

Uthman sent to every Muslim province one copy of what they had copied, and ordered that all the other Qur'anic materials, whether written in fragmentary manuscripts or whole copies, be burnt.[5]

It is the one he ordered Zaid and his editorial board to edit that eventually became the "Authorized Version" of the Qur'an. Uthman destroyed the other people's texts, not because they were un-authentic; all he did was to make sure that only one codex remained. This, basically, was to prevent different sects from springing up because of different texts. It was a political decision. If people divided in doctrine because of differing versions of the Qur'an, they would soon be politically polarized, and this could

[4] Jeffery, Arthur, *Materials for the History of the Text of the Qur'an* (New York: AMS Press, 1975) pp. 24-114.
[5] *Sahih Al-Bukhari*, Vol. 6, #510.

weaken the Islamic political power. That's why various codices were destroyed. Therefore, the present authorized Uthman version is the politically correct Qur'an.

The Hadith says the Qur'an was divinely revealed to Muhammad in seven dialects. Why then did Uthman decide to standardize it in only one dialect?

Some modern Muslims, who believe it is their duty to defend the Qur'an at all costs, abandoning what history says, claim that the Qur'an had no different versions, no variant reading, and no conflicting manuscripts. Some of them say versions existed but the differences were insignificant. But if the differences were insignificant, why the changes, why the standardization and why should the other versions be burnt? Someone said the versions were destroyed in order "...to ensure uniformity," even though the same writer denies the existence of other versions.

But soon after this "Authorized Version" of the Qur'an came out, protests arose from different quarters stating that certain portions that were obviously recited by Muhammad when he was alive were not in this "Authorized King Uthman Version." When the Shi'ite[6] sect emerged later, members accused Uthman that about twenty-five percent of the authentic material in the Qur'an was destroyed in order to undermine the doctrinal and political beliefs of the Shi'ites.[7]

---

[6] "Shiat Ali" means party of Ali or supporters of Ali's political ambition to the leadership of the Islamic ondition.

[7] *McClintock and Strong's Cyclopedia of Biblical, Theological and Ecclesiastical Literature* (Grand Rapids: Baker Book House, 1981) Vol. 5, p. 152.

Even Aisha, Muhammad's widow, who was also instrumental in the gathering of some of the shreds that were compiled, had remembered AFTER the "Authorized Version" had come out that there were certain portions she knew existed when Muhammad was alive that were obviously missing in the new text. Those missing portions remain missing, even today. Aisha is also quoted as saying:

> "The verse of the stoning, and of sucking an adult ten times were revealed, and they were (written) on a paper and kept under my bed. When the messenger of Allah expired and we were preoccupied with his death, a goat entered and ate away the paper."

This is recorded by Abu Muslim, Ibn Maja, and Ibn Qutbah.[8]

A Shia Islamic website quotes several Islamic Hadith writers as saying that:

> "… a sheet on which two verses, including that on stoning, were recorded were under her (Ai'sha's) bedding and that after the Prophet died, a domestic animal got into the room and gobbled up the sheet while the household was preoccupied with his funeral."[9]

If Aisha's report is true (and we have no reason to doubt it since she was the wife closest to Muhammad) we can be

---

[8] Ibn Qutbah, Tawil Mukhtalafi 'l-Hadith (Cairo: Maktaba al-Kulliyat al-Azhariyya. 1966) page 310.
[9] www.al-islam.org/encyclopedia/shia8/txt

sure that the sura that was "gobbled up" by an animal has been lost forever. That was part of the "original Qur'an."

After this "standardized" version had been sent to Muslim provinces as the most perfect, the Editor-in-Chief himself, Zaid, suddenly recalled some stories he had heard Muhammad recite when he was alive and which were not included in this final work. Later, he confessed:

> "A verse from Surat Ahzab was missed by me when we copied the Qur'an and I used to hear Allah's Apostle reciting it. So we searched for it and found it with Khuzaima-bin-Thabit al Ansari."[10]

How are we sure there were no other portions with other people that were not remembered? Even Umar, who had originally advised the compilation and editing, also discovered (after the first attempt of compilation) that something was still wrong. He observed that the portion on stoning an adulterer, which Muhammad often recited, was missing from the present work. They did not include this omission. Today, that portion (*ayat ul-rajm*), is still missing from the Qur'an which Muslims carry around as a complete Qur'an.[11]

Writers like Abul A'ala Maududi, in his translation of the Qur'an, *The Meaning of the Qur'an*, as well as in his *Introduction to Yusuf Ali's English translation of the Qur'an*, have been trying to rescue the Qur'an from the facts of

---

[10] *Sahih Al-Bukhari*, Vol. 6. Book 61, #510.
[11] Ibn Ishaq, *Sirat Rasul*, p. 684; *Sahih Muslim*, Book 17, #4194; Sahih Bukhari, Vol. 8, Book 82, #816, 817; Vol. 9, Book 92, #424; Vol. 9, Book 93, #633.

the history of the book. But these facts are too strong to be wished away. It is also significant that the portion on the compilation of the Qur'an in al Bukhari's Hadith was completely omitted by the University of California Muslim Students Association on their website.[12]

Mirza Muhsin has pointed out that a whole sura known as *Surat'n Nurain* was deliberately expunged by the final compilers of the Qur'an.

Shi'ite Muslims have also consistently alleged that portions of even the present Qur'an are wrong. These are the areas where they believe the Qur'an is speaking of Ali or their beliefs concerning the authority and succession of Imams.

Shi'ite books that allege that the present Qur'an circulating among Muslims is grossly corrupted include: *The Mirror of Minds* by Al-Majlisi, *The Corruption* by Ahmad Ibn Muhammad, *Corruption And Substitution* by Muhammad Ibn Hassan Al-Sairafi, and *The Abridgment on the Corruption of the Book of the Lord of Lords* by Imam Al-Nuri.

Other Shi'ite scholars who have conclusively established the case of corruption of the present Qur'an are Al-Ayaashi, Al-Kalleeni, Ali Ibn Ibrahim, Al-Saduuq, Al-Numaani, to mention only the most notable.

Ali ibn Abi Taalib also made his own collection. His was more on the side of the Shi'ite persuasion.

Ubayy ibn Kab's version was in circulation in Syria. This version has two more suras than the Uthman version. The

---

12 www.usc.edu/dept/MSA/fundamentals/hadithsunnah/bukhari/

two suras were *Surat al-Hafd* and *Surat al-Khaf*. Al-Bai-haqi wrote that these two suras were authentic and were being used in prayer by Khalif Umar ibn Al-Khataab (successor of Abu Bakr). There is a version where the first chapter is not al Fatiha as we have it today.

Ibn Masu'd, one of the best reciters of the Qur'an, whom Muhammad himself recommended, had his own version. This version did not include Suras 1, 113 and 114, which we have in the modern Qur'an.

A Traditionalist, Abu Musa, quoted Al-Ah'ari as telling a group of reciters of the Qur'an at Basrah:

> "Verily, we used to recite a sura which in length and severity we used to compare to Bara'ah and I have forgotten it, except that I remember of it *(the words)* 'Ye relied' etc. And we used to recite a sura which we were wont to compare with one of the Rosaries, and I have forgotten it, except that of it I remember *(the words)*, 'O ye who', etc."

The *Surat Bara'ah* (i.e. Sura 9) is 130 verses long (129 in Al-Hilali et al). The first lost sura here is said to be as long as this Sura 9. That means a sura of about 130 verses is lost to a failed memory! There were two of such suras.

Moreover, Muhammad's widow, Aisha, is quoted as saying that the sura that was named *al Saff* (present Sura 61) had 200 verses when Muhammad was alive. After the mass destruction and the revision by Uthman, only 72 verses survived. Today, only 14 verses remain in that sura!

In his book *The Abridgment On The Corruption Of The Book Of The Lord of Lords* referred to earlier, Shi'ite scholar

Imam Al-Nuri says that in an earlier version of the Qur'an (which he believes is more authentic), *Surat Baiyina* (Sura 98) was also as long as *Surat al Baqara* (Sura 2), which has 286 verses. In the present version of the Qur'an, that sura has only eight verses!

The Abrogation Question

Is there evidence that even at the time of Muhammad the Qur'an was being changed? We shall answer that question from the Qur'an itself:

> "Allah blots out what He will and confirms what He will. And with Him is the Mother of the Book."[13]

This is the theory in Islamic doctrine called abrogation. The theory is that Allah can reveal something today and later cancel it as not exactly correct or expedient and bring a better revelation tomorrow or months after. On this issue of abrogation, the Qur'an is its own judge. Allah explains this theory:

> "Such of our revelations as We abrogate or cause to be forgotten, We bring *(in place)* one better or like thereof. Knowest thou not that Allah is able to do all things?"[14]

God can, indeed, do all things. But the real God, the God of the Bible, has limited Himself by His character of holiness, integrity and trustworthiness. He cannot tell a lie. He does not give an instruction today and knock it out of one's memory or deny it tomorrow.

---

13 Sura 13:39
14 Sura 2:106

> "And if We will, We could take away that which
> We have sent to you by inspiration. Then you
> would find no pleader for you against Us in that
> respect"[15]

Were this statement taken from a secular history book,
one might say that it was an attack from the enemies of
Islam intended to disparage the religion, and some Muslim leaders might incite a jihad against the person.

The true God cannot change His word because His
Word is perfect. It is NOT an imperfect thing that needs
modifications. As King, God weighs His words before
speaking them, and therefore cannot make frivolous
changes. In the Bible, God Himself said:

> "My covenant will I not break, nor alter the thing
> that is gone out of my lips."[16]

If Allah changes his words any time he feels like, one
must ask if those words were ever perfect. And how do we
trust the new substitutes?

A wise person will only trust an unchanging God. If
God promised us something today, He won't change it
tomorrow. We can trust Him because we can trust His
Word. That was why He called on the children of Israel,
especially those who began to turn to idols:

> Produce your cause *(present your case)*, saith the
> LORD; bring forth your strong reasons," saith the
> King of Jacob.[17]

---

[15] Sura 17:86
[16] Psalm 89:34 (See also Isaiah 34:16)
[17] Isaiah 41:21

God was here challenging His people to bring forth any word He had at any time ever spoken to them by which they could plead their case before Him, as in a court of law. Has He ever failed them or their fathers who served Him faithfully? This is wonderful. Our God is a God of justice and faithfulness. He will never contradict or change His words.

Several people in the Bible took God up on certain issues. They argued certain cases out with God. When we are in a personal relationship with Him, God takes time to reason with us at our level. Abraham subtly brought forth his strong reasons why God should not destroy the whole of Sodom and Gomorrah (so that his kinsman, Lot, and his household could be saved). Moses argued that the Lord, based on His earlier promises to their grandfathers, should not exterminate Israel because of their apostasy.[18] Many other prophets took God at His word when praying.

That is what many of us Christians do. We quote God to present our cases before Him. No, we are not arrogant before Him. We relate with Him as His children, and it is based on that relationship that we pray—based on what He has spoken in His Word. God says:

> "Put me in remembrance: let us plead together: declare thou, that thou mayest be justified *(acquitted)*."[19]

Unfortunately, this is exactly what Allah seems not to

---

[18] Exodus 14-32:11
[19] Isaiah 43:26

allow in Sura 17:86. He says he obliterates part of his constitution anytime he wants to, *"Lest you find anything against Us."*

Many Arabs would not be taken for a ride. Although they might be illiterate, they were no fools. They asked if such arbitrary substitution and elimination from a supposedly divine revelation do not make the claim of revelation suspect. And so we have this revelation from Muhammad to justify such actions:

> "When We *(Allah)* substitute (or change) one revelation *(verse)* for another -- and Allah knows best what He reveals, - they say, 'Thou art a forger': But most of them understand not."[20]

Here, these Arabians were saying to Muhammad, "Thou art a forger." Our question is: Were these people right? Apart from the constant canceling of revelations by Allah, did Muhammad also forge certain revelations on some occasions and regard them as coming from Allah in heaven?

Let us not speculate. Let Allah answer. He told Muhammad:

> "Indeed they were near to seducing thee from that *(which)* We revealed to thee, that thou mightest *forge* against Us *another*, and then they would surely have taken thee as a friend."[21]

This means what it says, that "The people almost seduced you (Muhammad) from the revelation we (Allah)

---

[20] Sura 16:101
[21] Sura 17:75

gave you, so that you might forge against us another revelation, or so that you might bring another revelation from yourself and claim it came from us (Allah); by doing this, you would have won the friendship of these idolaters." Read this verse from the Qur'an again.

Our interest is in the words "forge" and "another." There can be no "another" unless there was an earlier forging. While Allah was revealing and withdrawing, his apostle was also doing something.

At the rate at which "revelations" were coming and were being abrogated and substituted, blotted out, forgotten and replaced, it is clear that if Muhammad had not died when he did, he would have continued receiving more revelations and would have continued erasing and substituting the old ones he had received. Muhammad did not expect to die in the year he did. Those who have read the Qur'an to the end will notice that it does not have a conclusion.

So if a revelation was given two years ago, and today it is destroyed and replaced with another, which of the two can we call the original, the one on "the Mother of Books" in heaven? Gerhard Nehls wrote:

> "We suggest that Allah could have spared us a lot of confusion, doubt and explaining, had He given the better text right from the beginning."[22]

Maybe we should point out one or two examples of the abrogated revelations. The author of the Qur'an says:

---

[22] Nehls, Gerhard, *Christians Ask Muslims*, (Nairobi: Life Challenge Africa, 1992) p.14.

"....Take as your place of worship where Abraham stood to pray...." [23]

By this he meant Ka'aba in Mecca. When Muhammad fled to Medina (where a majority of Jews lived), he told them that his religion was the same as that of the Jewish ancestors. Since Jews faced Jerusalem while praying, he said he now received a new portion of the Qur'an from Allah that shows that the true worshippers must be facing Jerusalem while praying.

Jews were studying him to see if they should support his religion. When he saw they were not cooperating, he told his followers that he just received another revelation which says there is no worship in having to face a particular direction in prayer since Allah has every place:

"Unto Allah belong the East and West; and whithersoever ye turn, there is Allah's countenance." [24]

In other words, a Muslim could face any direction to pray. His followers were confused at this level.

However, when he fully took control of Medina and subjugated the Jews, and later conquered Mecca, he said he had received another revelation which says all true worshippers *must* face the shrine of Ka'aba in Mecca while praying, if their prayer would be answered. [25] All these revelations and counter-revelations are in the same Sura 2!

In Sura 2:142-145, Muhammad's followers questioned why he had to change the *kibla* (the direction of prayer)

[23] Sura 2:125

[24] Sura 2:115 (Pickthall)

[25] Sura 2:142-145

again. His answer was that they were foolish for asking such a question.

In abrogation, many old revelations were destroyed; but it is not all the abrogated revelations that were destroyed. Many of the abrogated verses were still not yet destroyed before Muhammad died. Therefore, many of the present verses of the Qur'an have been abrogated by other verses in the same Qur'an.

Scholars have pointed out that not less than two hundred and twenty five verses in the present Qur'an have been abrogated by other verses. Jalalu'd-Din is quoted in the *Dictionary of Islam* as saying the number of abrogated verses ranges between 5 and 500.[26]

Moreover, since the Qur'an claims to be eternal and to have "descended" from heaven, and that the original copy has long been there in heaven, why all the corrections by Allah? A thing that is eternal and perfect cannot be corrected. Does the abrogation affect the original in Paradise?

The Bible has been tried by people and it stands them all. God will not change His word because of man's criticism:

> "The words of the LORD are pure words: as silver tried in a furnace of earth, purified seven times"[27]

Anything calling itself "the Word of God" must be tried in the crucible. If it does not stand the test of criticism,

---

[26] *Dictionary of Islam*, p. 520; Abrogation is treated in more detail in the author's book, *My Reply: A Conversation With a Muslim Scholar*.
[27] Psalm 12:6

it must give way. A divine revelation must not be afraid of criticism. Why is it that Muslims are very much afraid when Islam, especially the Qur'an, is put under a microscope? Many Islamic leaders don't even like Christians reading the Qur'an or having access to their Hadith for fear of criticism. Interestingly, I know some Islamic bookshops who do not like selling the Qur'an or Hadith to someone they know is a Christian. Why? C.G. Pfander once wrote:

> "Pure gold has no reason to fear any test that can be applied to it, but comes out uninjured and approved from all kinds of testing and from the hottest fire"[28]

Memory Without the Holy Spirit

Jesus Christ knew that Middle Easterners had good memories, yet He did not commit His teachings to mere memories of man. The Bible says, "The heart is deceitful above all things..."[29] The Lord Jesus, therefore, promised His disciples the Holy Spirit whom He said would:

> "teach you all things, and bring all things to your remembrance, whatsoever I have said unto you."[30]

The disciples of Muhammad remembered certain areas that were part of the Qur'an only *after the final editing had been done*. The Islamic leaders did not want to add anything else so as to give an impression of sanctity to the book. How many more of such forgotten verses are still

---

[28] The Mizan-ul-Haqq, *Balance of Truth*, enl. (Villach: Light of Life, 1986) p. 280.
[29] Jeremiah 17:9
[30] John 14:26

not remembered till the death of these people? We do not know. As we have noted, some of the people who could have lived to remember anything had died in Jihad even before the editing and compilation started. *It is therefore clear from here that the claim of the "original copy" of the Qur'an existing today is a myth.*

Whose Voice Do We Hear in the Qur'an?

To a Muslim, that question is unnecessary. To him, Allah is the one speaking in the Qur'an. The words there are not the words of man, not the words of a historian or a prophet. In his book, *Is the Bible God's Word?*, Ahmed Deedat boasts of what he calls "three grades of evidence."[31] These three grades, he says, are words of God, words of a prophet of God, and words of a historian. According to him and many of his ilk, all the words in the Qur'an are words of Allah. Only the Qur'an contains purely the words of God, while the Bible is merely "an encyclopedia" of many historians and words of certain prophets.

Therefore, for a Muslim, Allah is the only one speaking throughout the Qur'an. It is not the word of Muhammad or any prophet or historian. As far as Deedat is concerned, the Bible is of no historical value, containing hearsay (unlike his own Hadith and the Qur'an).

We will not examine the Hadith here, but a quote from one of the Hadith will clarify this issue of the historical worth of this Islamic "history." In the Hadith *Mishkat'ul Masabih* we read the words of at-Termeze (also spelled Tirmize) one of the authorities of the history of Islam:

---

[31] Deedat, Ahmed, *Is the Bible God's Word?*, p. 6.

> "Abu Kuraib said of us that Ibrahim-ibn-Yusif ibn Abi Ishaq said of us from his father, from Abu Ishaq, from Tulata-ibn-Musarif, that he said, 'I have heard, from Abdu'r Rahman-ibn-Ausajah that the Apostle of Allah said: 'Whoever shall give in charity a milch cow, or silver or a leathern bottle of water, it shall be equal to the freeing of a slave.'"[32]

That is just an example of the hearsay that runs through the Hadith, and which Muslims take as historical authority. Even though they cannot point out a story written in such a manner in the Bible, they regard the Bible as being in the same grade with the Hadith (if not lower), and the Qur'an far more superior because it contains "purely" the words of Allah.

There are too many cases we can cite in the Qur'an to throw away such claims. But let us point out a few:

> "And we descend not but by command of your Lord. To Him belongs what is before us, and what is behind us, and what is between those two and your Lord was never forgetful"[33]

This is obviously supposed to be an angel speaking. Both Yusuf Ali and Al-Hilali *et al*, in their translations of the Qur'an, indicate that the words are not the words of Allah but of "angels" which they rightly put in brackets to identify the "we" speaking in that sura. Not even one Angel Jubril, but "angels." The "we" there is different from

---

[32] Quoted in *Islam: A Challenge to Faith* by Samuel M. Zwemer (New York: Student Volunteer Movement for Foreign Missions, 1907), p. 101.
[33] Surah 19:64

"your Lord" there. Yet Islamic teachers want their pupils to believe that only the words of Allah are in the Qur'an, and those of Muhammad are in the Hadith, and other prophets, angels, etc. have their words in history books of Islamic writers.

In fact, we have more words of human beings in the Qur'an than direct words of Allah. Let a Muslim take one long sura in the Qur'an and find out for himself. When, for example, we have words of Abraham, Moses, Aaron, Mary, in the Qur'an, it amazes us that Islamic writers still brainwash their pupils that only the words of Allah are in their book. Or why should God be rehearsing the history of men which had already been documented and was in circulation?

Who is Speaking Here?

In the discourse of the Jinn (spirits) at a place called Taif, which is supposed to be Muhammad's encounter with some spirits in that place, we are told that these are also the Words of Allah. Yet this is a report of an experience *of Muhammad* when he first fled Mecca (before he ran to Medina). Is it Allah reporting to Muhammad what Muhammad himself experienced? Let us see part of the message of these jinn:

> "... Verily, we have heard a wonderful Recitation (this Qur'an)! 2) It guides to the Right Path, and we have believed therein, and we shall never join (in worship) anything with our Lord (Allah). 3) And He exalted is the Majesty of our Lord, has taken neither a wife nor a son (or offspring or children).

4) And that the foolish among us [i.e. Iblis (Satan) or the polytheist amongst the jinn] used to utter against Allah that which was an enormity in falsehood. 5) And verily, we thought that men and jinn would not utter a lieu against Allah.

6) And Verily, there were men among mankind who took shelter with the males among the jinn, but they (jinn) increased them (mankind) in sin and transgression. 7) And they thought as you thought, that Allah will not send any Messenger (to mankind or jinn).

8) And we have sought to reach the heaven, but found it filled with stern guards and flaming fires. 9) And verily, we used to sit there in stations, to (steal) a hearing, but any who listens now will find a flaming fire watching him in ambush.

10) And we know not whether evil is intended for those on earth, or evil is intended for those on earth, or whether their Lord intends for them a Right Path. 11) There are among us some that are righteous, and some the contrary; we are groups having different ways (religious sects). 12) And we think that we cannot escape Him by flight.

13) And indeed when we heard the Guidance (this Qur'an), we believed therein (Islamic Monotheism), and whosoever believes in his Lord shall have no fear, either of a decrease in the reward of his good deeds or an increase in the punishment for his sins.

14) And of us some are Muslims (who have submitted to Allah, after listening to this Qur'an), and
of us some are Al-Qasitun (disbelievers – those
who have deviated from the Right Path)'. And
whosoever has embraced Islam (i.e. has become a
Muslim by submitting to Allah), then such have
sought the Right Path."

15) And as for the Qasitun (disbelievers who deviated from the Right Path), they shall be fire-
wood for Hell.[34]

These are spirits who confess they have been cast out of
heaven, but now they are converted to Islam and have become Muslims (verses 13 and 14). After they left heaven,
they were still making attempts to peep.

"And verily, we used to sit there (in heaven) to
(steal) a hearing, but anyone who listens now will
find a flaming fire watching him in ambush..."
(verse 9).

The Bible clearly identifies these spirits as demons and
not angels of God. Holy angels do not peep into heaven.
These are the ones speaking in chapter 72 of the Qur'an.
The chapter is actually titled Al-Jinn (The Jinn). [35]

Verse 19 of that Sura says, "When the slave of Al-lah
(Muhammad) stood up invoking (Allah) in prayer they
(the jinn) just made round him a dense crowd as if stick-
ing one over the other (in order to listen to the Prophet's

---

[34] Sura 72:1-15
[35] For further on the discourse of these jinn in the Qur'an, read the
author's book, *My Reply: A Conversation With A Muslim Scholar.*

recitation)." Does a crowd of jinn still hover around a mosque when Allah is being invoked today? Since jinn love to listen to the recitation of the Qur'an, do they come round when a Muslim recites from the Qur'an?

Sura 46:29-32 also shows a set of jinn whom Allah sent to Muhammad to listen to the recitation of the Qur'an. As they heard it, they not only became Muslims, they became Muslim 'evangelists' among the other jinn, recruiting more jinn into Islam.

Apart from these "jinnic verses" in the Qur'an, there is a strange verse that should make a serious Muslim think. Allah says:

> "Never did We send a Messenger or a Prophet before you but when he did recite the revelation or narrated or spoke, Shaitan (Sa-tan) threw (some falsehood) in it. But Allah abolishes that which Shaitan (Satan) throws in. Then Allah establishes His Revelations. And Allah is All-Knower, all-Wise. That He (Al-lah) may make what is thrown in by Shaitan (Satan) a trial for those in whose hearts is a disease and whose hearts are hardened. ..."[36]

These verses say that a prophet of Allah should expect that once in awhile he could have a few verses from Satan interjected in what he presents to people as revelations. Allah would allow those verses to try some people and then later abolish them. How many of such verses were slotted into the original Qur'an (and then abolished) we

---

[36] Sura 22:52-53 (Al-Hilali)

do not know. Whether or not all of them were abolished before the sudden death of the prophet we do not know.

We have seen some of the things the Qur'an suffered at its compilation. What about the history of its "descent" from heaven? Is there an evidence of a human finger in its composition? This we shall examine next.

4

Who Taught Muhammad?

Doubts of Arabians

Many intelligent people who study the Qur'an wonder how Arabs could believe in the divine authorship or descent of the book from heaven, sura by sura.

A careful student of the Qur'an will see that Arabians were not fools, and not altogether gullible. Many were, and still are, really intelligent. They are not complaining today because their leaders have subjugated them intellectually. Those who are not under strict Islamic control have a degree of freedom to question their religion. But most would still not do so for fear.

Many times when Muhammad said that a sura had just descended from heaven, many Arabs suspected something was fishy. And so we have this verse:

"Whenever there cometh down a surah, they look at each other, (Saying), "Doth anyone see you (when it was coming down from heaven)? Then they turn aside: Allah hath turned their hearts (from the light): for they are a people that understand not."[1]

The Jabr Connection

"We know indeed that they say, 'It is a man that teaches him.' The tongue of him they wickedly point to is notably foreign, while this is Arabic, pure and clear."[2]

The "man that teaches him" is a young "Christian"[3] friend of Muhammad called Jabr, whom Muhammad always visited at Marwah Quarters, not too far from his house. The allegation was that when Muhammad visited Jabr and heard the stories of the Bible, some were put on record. People believed that Muhammad usually presented these parchments and claimed he had received them hot from heaven through the angel Gabriel.

Muhammad refuted this strong allegation through another "revelation" from "Gabriel." The defense was that since Jabr was of "a foreign tongue" (he was not an Arab by birth), he could not have taught Muhammad anything. But it does not matter if Jabr was a non-Arab. Since he had stayed long in Arabia, he could have known Arabic very well and related his stories to Muhammad in good Arabic. How could Jabr be a close friend of Muhammad (if he did not understand Arabic) since Muhammad did

---

[1] Sura 9:127

[2] Sura 16:103

[3] People and movements labeled "Christian" in this book are usually referring to a ritualistic religion with roots in Catholicism.

not understand any other language? We must realize too that Muhammad's main Secretary was a Jew. According to Muslim writer Muhammad Haykal, Muhammad...

> "had chosen him (the Secretary) for his capacity to write letters in Hebrew and Syriac as well as Arabic. After the evacuation of Jews from Madinah, the Prophet no longer trusted a non-muslim to write his letters."

That means, too, that the Jewish background of Jabr could not be a plausible reason why he couldn't have helped Muhammad in his collection of what is now called the Qur'an. If Muhammad's own Secretary was of "a foreign tongue" and yet well versed in Arabic, Syriac and his own Hebrew language, then it is not inconceivable to get Hebrew scriptures and literature interpreted and translated into Arabic by the Secretary. Since the Secretary was such a brilliant fellow and was versatile in these three languages, therefore, the alleged brilliance of the language of the Qur'an is not a necessary and sufficient proof of heavenly authorship. Rather, it can be a reflection of the brilliance of Jabr, since Muhammad is believed to have been illiterate.

Pure Arabic?

In the verse in question, the only defense the Qur'an gives against the charge of an outside human finger is that the Qur'an was "pure Arabic" while the alleged secret finger was foreign. However, it is not even true that the Qur'an is purely Arabic. What does "Pure Arabic" mean? At what linguistic level is the Arabic of the Qur'an pure, lexically, syntactically or even phonologically? Lexically, no. There are many Persian, Syriac, Hebrew, old Egyptian, Assyrian and Greek words in the Arabic Qur'an. Arthur Jeffery[4] has pointed out over one hundred non-Arabic words in the Arabic Qur'an. Jalalu's-Din As-Syuti also identifies one hundred and seven non-Arabic words. So where is the lexical purity?

Syntactically or grammatically, the Qur'an has many problems, some of which we shall touch in the next chapter. Phonologically, the Qur'an is said by Muhammad to have been revealed in seven dialects or readings (sab'at-I-ahruf). In the Hadith Sahih Bukhari, Muhammad said:

> "The Qur'an has been revealed to be recited in seven different ways, so recite of it whichever is easy for you."[5]

The same Hadith quotes Muhammad as saying:

> "Gabriel taught me to recite in one style. I replied to him and kept asking him to give more (styles), till he reached seven modes (of recitation)."[6]

Since dialectal differences are usually in pronunciation, and the Qur'an can be recited in different dialects, there is no particular standard to judge the purity of the Qur'an on the phonological level. Therefore, the claim that the book descended in pure Arabic is defeated.

Since it gave the "purity" of its Arabic as the evidence

---

[4] Jeffery, A., *The Foreign Vocabulary of the Qur'an* (Lahore: Al-Biruni, 1977).
[5] See Hadith *Sahih Al-Bukhari*, Vol. 9, #640 and Vol. 6, #514.
[6] Hadith *Sahih Al-Bukhari*, Book 4, #1785.

of its divine inspiration, and this "evidence" has been disproved, the claim of the divine origin therefore falls on the ground.

The use of many foreign words, rather than supporting Muhammad's defense, is strong evidence to the contrary, indicating that the mysterious finger behind the Qur'an is that of a man who knew more than one language.

Badawi and Zamakshari admit that even the word Injil (referring to the gospel) is not an Arabic word but a Syriac word used by Christians before Muhammad started his religion.

Many committed Muslims do not want to believe that Muhammad's "visions" could have been obtained from other sources. They do not want to believe that quite a number of people who surrounded him were acquainted with the stories in the Bible. History is not on the side of such modern Muslims.

Older Muslim scholars knew better. From a number of Islamic books, we gather that Muhammad was surrounded by many Christians—even if nominal. One of them was Waraqa ibn Naufal, the cousin of Khadija, Muhammad's wife. One of his wives, Umm Habbibah, was formerly the wife of a Christian, Ubaidu'llah ibn Jahsh. Another wife of Muhammad, Miriam, and her sister, Sirin, were Christian slaves given to Muhammad. Biographer Ibn Ishaq records that Abdu'llah ibn Salam (one of the best reciters of the Qur'an) was a seasoned Jewish Rabbi before he became a Muslim and personal friend of Muhammad. Some scholars say "the other man" alleged in Sura 16:103 as tutoring Muhammad could be this ibn Salam.

No respectable scholar can deny that Muhammad was surrounded by many people learned in Jewish and Persian religions. Other Islamic scholars like Abbasi have identified many Christians who were strongly believed to have influenced the composition of the Qur'an.

There was, for example, a Greek Christian whose Arabic name was Abu Takbihah, as well as a male Christian slave Yasar (otherwise known as Abu Fuqaihah). The Arabians said these people helped Muhammad write those "sheets" he often brought as revelations which allegedly came hot from the throne of God, and were brought by the angel Jubril (Gabriel):

> "Whenever revelation comes, they say... who was there with you...?"

This accusation of the Arabians is recorded further:

> "Those who disbelieve say: 'This is nothing but a lie that he has invented and others have helped him at it, so that they have produced an unjust wrong (thing) and a lie.'"

And they say: "Tales of the ancients, which he has had written down: and they are dictated to him morning and afternoon."

Say: "The (Qur'an) was sent down by Him who knows the mystery (that is) in the heavens and the earth: verily He is Oft-Forgiving, Most Merciful"[7]

Such is the case brought up in Sura 16:103. The man suspected of giving other literary help to Muhammad in

---

[7] Sura 25:4-5 (Al-Hilali); 25:6 (Ali)

Sura 25 is a man identified by Abbasi as Cain, or Yasar or our friend Jabr as others have opined and as we have hinted above. Other people whose names were given were a monk, Addas, and Salman, Suhaib, and of course, Muhammad's Secretary, who had a Christian background. In fact, the case of Jabr was so known to people in Mecca that they began to mock Jabr as the "Holy Spirit" or "Angel Gabriel" from whom Muhammad was receiving some of his revelations.

On Plagiarism

The influences noted above are not just in hearing stories and having them jotted down as revelations. There are hints of outright plagiarism identified by scholars. But, interestingly, we have a serious challenge concerning the sacredness and originality of the Qur'an:

> "And if you are in doubt as to which We (Allah) have revealed to Our servant (Muhammad), then produce a chapter like it, and call on your helper, besides Allah, if you are truthful."[8]

Most Arabs were illiterate at that time. Moreover, many of the original works from which Arabs could have discovered the sources of Qur'an material were in foreign languages. Informed scholars now laugh at such a challenge since clear evidence now exists to establish outright plagiarism in the Qur'an. We will now cite a few of these.

It has been established that verses 1, 29, 31 and 46 of Sura 54 (Surat al-Qamar) were lifted from a poem of a

[8] Sura 2:23

pre-Islamic Arabic poet, Imraul Qais.[9] Even at the time of Muhammad, some sneered at the challenge to "produce a chapter like it." For example, the poet Imraul Qais' daughter was still alive when Muhammad started his religion. One day this lady was listening to Muhammad reciting the "revelations" he had just received hot from heaven from his Angel Jubril. She recognized the verses from her father's poems, and stood aghast and amused, wondering how these could be a revelation written by Allah and preserved in the "Preserved Tablet" in heaven from before the creation of the world!

Another time, this lady met Fatima, Muhammad's daughter, reciting the first verse of Surat Qamar. Qais' daughter said:

> "Oh that is what your father has taken from my father's poems ("Mollaqat") and calls it something that has come down to him from heaven!"

If the original works of a secular Arab poet could be seen in the Qur'an, then it is scarcely of any use to maintain the claim that the Qur'an is so wonderful that the most learned Arab or even a spirit could not produce its kind.[10]

The story of Abraham, as recorded in Sura 37:83-99, is not found in the Bible. This story was actually lifted from a Jewish collection of folktales titled, *Midrash Rabbah*. This book was in circulation 400 years before the Qur'an was written. Since most Arabs were illiterate at that time

---

[9] St. Clair-Tisdall, *The Original Sources of the Qur'an* (London: Society for Promoting Christian Knowledge (SPCK), 1905) p. 25.
[10] Sura 17:88; Sura 2:23 (Al-Hilali)

and the book was not in wide circulation in Mecca or in the Arabic language, the authors of the Qur'an did not know that this plagiarism would be discovered.

The Bible records that the Lord Jesus was born in a manger. The Qur'an says He was born under a palm tree. Sura 19:29-30 speaks of a one-day-old baby Jesus speaking in the cradle. These errors did not originate in the Qur'an. They were lifted from an Arabic apocryphal fable written in Egypt titled *First Gospel of the Infancy of Jesus Christ.* The original fable says:

> "... Jesus spake even when he was in the cradle, and said: 'Mary, I am Jesus the son of God. That word which thou didst bring forth according to the declaration of the angel...'"

In the Qur'an, however, the expression "son of God" was changed to "slave (or servant) of God." We don't know why.

There is also the story of a young Jesus making a live bird out of clay. There is no biblical basis for such a story. But this story is found to have been culled from the anthology of fables called *'Gospel of Infancy"* referred to above. Several of such stories abound. The Qur'an says:

> "Yet they ask thee to hasten on the punishment! But God will not fail in His promise. Verily, a day in the sight of thy Lord is like a thousand years of your reckoning."[11]

This is a plagiarism from 2 Peter 3:3, 4, 8. The last statement can also be found in Psalms 84:10 and 90:4.

---

[11] Sura 22:47

We are amused that some Muslims claim the Bible is not the Word of God because it has names of human authors. Why then did the Qur'an copy from it? A Muslim may protest that their prophet never copied anything from the Bible. However, the Qur'an says Muhammad should:

> "Copy the guidance they (the Jews and Christians) received"[12]

And he did copy it!

We have no grudge against the writer of the Qur'an for copying something from our holy book. Our problem is that he copied wrongly and claimed it to be the original! Now, why should Muslims claim that the Bible is not the Word of God but words of men? If it is not the Word of God, why do you "borrow" from it—borrow the words of men, like Peter, David, and others to include in your "Word of God"?

It is because of the foregoing that we have question marks on the claims of originality and divine authorship which were made in Sura 10:37-38.

---

[12] Sura 6:90 (Ali)

5

Critique of the Qur'an

MUSLIM leaders do not allow anybody to test or criticize the Qur'an. They see a critical evaluation as an attack on Islam. They scare their followers from any contact with Christian books on Islam. Many times, such books are bought in large quantities and burnt to prevent other Muslims from reading them.

Sometimes, Muslims threaten the government, threatening to riot if they do not do something. Some of them use their position in the police or secret police to harass Christian booksellers and publishers who distribute such books while they themselves publish and circulate anti-Christian books, audio, and videocassettes all over the world.

These efforts to prevent Muslims from reading Christian books are a sign of the weakness of Islam.

Muslim leaders are hiding something which they don't want their followers to know. This is intellectual captivity.

Looking at the Qur'an

Every morning in the mosque, the muezzin or the Imam calls us from the minaret, "Come, and accept Islam - the religion of success and enjoyment." Our response is, "Would you mind we sit down first and examine all the major claims of Islam before we consider coming?"

That will be an offense.

In places where they are free to bring their loudspeakers outside, Muslim Imams assault the minds of people every morning with their preaching; but they are afraid of hearing a Christian sermon.

The Qur'an considers itself to be perfect. It says there is no book like it in its perfection, and that no human being or even spirits can write such a book.[1]

Muslims have always maintained that their book has its original copy in heaven, and that the one they have now is a copy of the original in heaven. It is this claim of heavenly origin that has prevented many Muslims from a thorough analysis of the book; and we believe this does not help scholarship. No one should fear testing an excellent and perfect thing.

Many Westerners who have attempted to read the Qur'an have complained to me that they get discouraged because they cannot flow along with it. Only scholars and students who must study the book have been able to read through to the end, though not without some mental torture. The reason is that structurally, the Qur'an has many problems. A serious reader will discover that the book is

---

[1] Sura 17:88

not arranged with any particular logic. It is neither chronological nor thematically logical in any way. The stories and the instructions were gathered and compiled haphazardly without recourse to history or even simple logic. Even the chapters are not arranged according to the time they were written or "received" by Muhammad.

In an attempt to find an order for the book, some Muslims have claimed that the Qur'an was arranged according to the length of the suras. But this is not true. Sura 2 is the longest sura, and the last sura (114) is not the shortest. Suras 103, 108, 110, 112, 113, etc. are all shorter than Sura 114.

There is simply no order in the arrangement.

Even within a sura, many verses or sections have no link with one another. Sometimes a story begins in the middle and is still not complete at the "end." Some sentences are even incomplete. There is scarcely any complete story in the Qur'an. The whole of the book does not have a sense of completeness. It does not have a beginning or a conclusion. If the prophet of Islam had not died at the time he did, the Qur'an would have been more voluminous than it is presently. That is the reason for the absence of a conclusion.

Sura 66 is titled "Banning" but only five of the thirteen verses say anything about banning; and the banning is the threat of divorce of Muhammad's wives. Over 70% of that sura has nothing to do with its title. Sura 66, verse 5 warns Muslims to ward off the hell Fire, but we do not know what logical link verses 7 and 8 have with the instruction in verse 6. Verse 9 says another thing entirely; and verses

10 to 12 bring several events and people together who have no historical link. More on this will follow in the next chapter.

The same is true of several other suras in the Qur'an. Islamic theologian, Ali Dashti, has also observed this:

> "The Qur'an contains sentences which are incomplete and not fully intelligible without the aid of commentaries; ...adjectives and verbs inflected without observance of the concords of gender and number; illogically and ungrammatically applied pronouns which sometimes have no referent; and predicates which in rhymed passages are often remote from the subjects."[2]

The Concise Encyclopedia of Islam describes the Qur'an as of "disjointed and irregular character:[3]

Even Abul A'ala Maududi, who wrote the introduction to Yusuf Ali's English translation of the Qur'an, acknowledges the structural problems in the Qur'an and confesses:

> "...one topic follows the other without any apparent connection. Sometimes a new topic crops up in the middle of another without any apparent reason. The speaker and the addressees, and the direction of the address change without any notice."[4]

---

[2] Dashti, Ali, *23 Years: A Study of the Prophetic Career of Muhammad* (London: George Allen and Unwin, 1985) p. 48.
[3] *The Concise Encyclopedia of Islam*, p. 231.
[4] Abul A'ala Maududi, In Yusuf Ali, *The Holy Qur'an: Text, Translation and Commentary*, 1938, Introduction, p. 5.

Amazingly, instead of Maududi accepting this as literary puerility, he persuades himself that this is a form of the uniqueness of the Qur'an. Why should we try to rescue the reputation of a book believed to have come from heaven? Such efforts are unwarranted.

It is for this same reason that Maududi wrote his own commentary of the Qur'an, *The Meaning of the Qur'an*. We understand the reason for all these efforts. He and Yusuf Ali cannot imagine a book from heaven with such problems. In fact, their whole faith (and therefore their whole life, etc.) falls or stands on the claim of the divine origin of the Qur'an. So they must maintain that, despite clear evidence to the contrary, the book came from heaven. Yet, Maududi still wrote in the introduction to Yusuf Ali's translation:

> "Unlike conventional books, the Qur'an does not contain information, ideas and arguments about specific themes arranged in a literary order... The same subject is repeated in different ways and one topic follows the other without any apparent connection. Sometimes a new topic crops up in the middle of another without any apparent reason. The speaker and the addressees, and the direction of the address change without any notice. There is no sign of chapters and divisions anywhere. Historical events are presented but not as in history books."

It is significant to note here that this introduction of Maududi is now omitted from a present edition of Yusuf Ali's translation published by IPCI, Islamic Vision,

1999. Obviously, such appraisal by such a respected Islamic scholar is too embarrassing for the modern Muslim. Unfortunately, such Muslims think that their hatred for American and European policies must force them to believe anything about the Qur'an even if they cannot prove such things.

Grammatical Mistakes

Many grammatical mistakes have been pointed out in the Arabic Qur'an by a number of native Arabic scholars. Arab Christian Evangelist, Dr. Anis A. Shorrosh, has pointed out at least six grammatical blunders. Islamic theologian, Ali Dashti, says there are over one hundred grammatical aberrations. We are not talking about copyist errors or errors of translation, but errors in the Arabic copies of the Qur'an. A few of these errors are in Sura 10:177 & 192; Sura 3:59; Sura 4:162; Sura 5:69; Sura 7:160, Sura 20:66; Sura 13:28, and Sura 58:10.[5] The beginning of some chapters of the Qur'an have some letters translated as: Alif-Lâm-Mîm-Sâd. No Muslim, dead or alive, knows the meaning of this. Dr Al-Hilali and Muhsin Kahn say, "These letters are one of the miracles of the Qur'an, and none but Allah (alone) knows their meanings."[6] They would not admit it is meaningless!

Quite a number of Muslims are aware of the incoherence, ambiguity and general weakness of their highly honored book, but they dare not point this out for fear of persecution and possible punishment for "blaspheming"

5 Shorrosh, Anis A., *Islam Revealed: A Christian Arab's View of Islam* (Nashville: Thomas Nelson Publishers, 1988) p. 199-200.
6 Verse 1 of Suras 2, 3, 29, etc.

the sacred book. To cover up these problems, the commentaries of translators like Yusuf Ali are more voluminous than the Qur'an itself. All Muslim translators of the Qur'an have to insert many phrases and clauses in brackets in the text. There are many such confusing interpolations in Al-Hilali and Muhsin Khan's translation. ***It is a re-writing of the Qur'an to make it say what they want.*** It is clear to them that without such personal addition, the reader cannot make much sense of such verses—even with their separate comments. In fact, many Muslims are more interested in memorizing verses than trying to understand the book. Some have the whole book in their head (which I consider a very commendable discipline). Some do this with the aid of charms, and offer an animal sacrifice at the end of the memorization training.

Versification

Another structural problem a Western student of the Qur'an will meet is the non-uniformity in the versification. Even though Muslims claim there is no difference between one Qur'an and another in any part of the world, it is a known but undeclared fact that many translations differ in versification. For example, Sura 5 (Al Maida) has 123 verses in Yusuf Ali's text and translation, while the same sura in Muhammad Taqui-ud-Din Al-Hilali and Muhammad Muhsin Khan's version and that of Muhammad Marmaduke Pickthall each have 120 verses. A man comparing one version with others should be ready to face such disparities. That is why when a Qur'anic reference is given, the reader is expected to check three or more verses before and after the number quoted.

Qur'an Not Translatable!

Muslim leaders say the Qur'an is so holy and great that it is untranslatable. They say Arabic is God's own language since that is the language in which the Qur'an "descended." The divine quality of the book would be lost if it is translated into any other language. According to this theory, the Persian Qur'an is not the Qur'an; Urdu, Telugu, English, French and Dutch Qur'ans are not the Qur'an. Anyone who quotes from them is not quoting from the Qur'an.

Is it the book itself that says it cannot be translated? No. Was it Muhammad that said so? No. It is the modern Islamic scholars who say this because they do not want non-Arabic speaking people to know all they have to know in the book. It is an attempt to keep people in darkness. When one quotes the book in a language other than Arabic, they say, "That is not a correct Qur'an." Islamic priests prefer that the congregation depend on them to interpret the Qur'an. They do not realize that if the Qur'an cannot be translated, it cannot be interpreted either. Therefore all preaching in the mosques must be done in Arabic. When an Imam tells us in English what the Qur'an says, we must not believe him since he is interpreting, which is equivalent to translating.

If Islam is for the world as Muslims claim, the Qur'an must be for the world. But how can the world understand it when only a tiny fraction of the world speaks Arabic? The Bible is for the world, and it is at home in any language.

If all the big Muslim scholars cannot translate the

Qur'an accurately, that shows the level of their linguistic knowledge. If Arabic professors cannot translate the Qur'an, what are they professing?

Miracles of Muhammad

The Qur'an mentions several times that Muhammad came to prove his prophet-hood with "clear signs." Most Muslims know that Muhammad did no single miracle— at least none mentioned in the Qur'an. Yet the Qur'an talks much of the "clear signs" he showed, which he believed were sufficient for Arabians to believe his claim of prophet-hood. A psychological weapon is being employed here. With such repetition, people tended to accept that there were "clear signs" or "clear evidence," even though they did not see any. For want of any miracle or evidence, Yusuf Ali says:

> "The clear evidence was the holy prophet himself,
> his life, his personality, and his teaching." [7]

We will not comment on the "holy life" of Muhammad. No place in the Qur'an refers to Muhammad as holy. Of all the prophets listed in the Qur'an, only Jesus is said to be holy, righteous or faultless (Sura 19:19). Muhammad's book is our concern here. If the quality of the Qur'an is the "clear evidence" of his prophet-hood and the greatest miracle in Islam, we need to go deeper and allow the evidence to speak for itself.

---

[7] Yusuf Ali, Commentary No. 6223.

6

The Bible vs. The Qur'an

The "Out-of-Context" Escape Clause

Whenever Christian writers point out something in the Qur'an which requires serious thinking from the Muslim, some Muslims simply dismiss it by saying the quote was taken out of context. When something is quoted and the reference is given, the reader should refer to the source to see if the quote has been given out of context.

But does the Qur'an *have* any context—any indisputable context? Hardly any story is complete in any one sura. As we have already seen, some narratives begin from nowhere. Such stories have no context unless one goes to their origin, which may be in the Bible or any of the books of fables, which form part of the sources of the Qur'an material. For many stories, one has to depend on the speculations of Islamic commentators; and there are as many commentaries as there are commentators.

Many Muslims who hold the claim of "out of context," meaning for every critical analysis of the Qur'an, do not realize that the Qur'an is its own verdict.

Some Muslims even believe that no non-Muslim can ever understand the Qur'an. According to their reasoning, only Muslim sheikhs and Imams can understand and interpret the book properly. However, Suras 43:2; 27:1 and 15:1 openly state that the words of the Qur'an make things so clear and simple that anybody can understand them.

If you are a Muslim, go directly to the Qur'an for your references. Your chief Imam is not the solution. He has his own interpretation, which may not be the same as somebody else's. ***Remember, you are personally responsible to God for whatever you choose to believe.***

Those who claim that a non-Muslim cannot know the Qur'an do not realize that much of the serious research works on the Qur'an were done (and are being done) by non-Muslims, especially in democratic nations where there is freedom of independent thinking and scholarship, and freedom to express one's findings.

This fact has been observed by Bishop Frans Zegers of the Netherlands:

> "The West knows far more about Islam than the countries of Islam know of the west. From the very beginning, the west has studied Islam far more thoroughly, knowing even more about it than the people of Islam themselves. Even to this day, this is so. ...The weighing of facts, the freedom of

thinking is denied, yeah, even marked blasphemy
in Islamic society." [1]

We can say that much of the wrong teachings in the
Qur'an came out of the misunderstanding of Biblical
teachings and history by Muhammad. Muslims have re-
peatedly reminded us that their prophet was stark illiterate. If we agree with that claim, it then becomes clearer
why we have the literary problems in the book. Nobody
could therefore have bothered to judge the book with any
serious literary criteria. But when Muslim writers exalt
the Qur'an above the Bible, flaunting the Holy Writ as
nothing and the Qur'an as superior, we now have a duty
to examine the Qur'an's literary worth.

Take, for example, the claim of the angels and Iblis
(Satan) being commanded by God to worship Adam as
recorded in several places in the Qur'an.[2] This is a misunderstanding of Hebrews 1:6 and Psalm 97:7 in the Bible.

The Qur'an and the Fall of Adam

The fall of Adam in the Garden of Eden is grossly
misunderstood by the writer of the Qur'an. Where was
Adam created? The Bible says Eden, the garden of God.
But where was this Eden? The author of the Qur'an felt
that since the Jews and the Christians talked of Adam
"falling," it meant falling from a height—falling from
heaven down to the planet earth. Allah is quoted in the
Qur'an as saying to Adam and Eve:

---

[1] Zegers, F.J.L., Protest letter to BBC about a documentary program
on Islam accusing the West of total ignorance of Islam. March 24, 1991.
Obtain a copy from Postbus 2171, Den Helder, 1780 BE Netherlands.
[2] Sura 2:34; Sura 7:11ff; Sura 15:28-35; Sura 20:116

"Get ye down (all ye people) with enmity between yourselves. On earth will be your dwelling place and your means of livelihood for a time."[3]

Here it is implied that Adam was created in heaven, and then thrown down when he sinned. We wish to point out to all Muslims that Adam did not fall "down" as the Qur'an supposes. God created this wonderful planet Earth to be inhabited by man and for man to enjoy and admire all the beautiful things He created.[4] So our being here on earth is not a punishment or as a result of the "fall" of Adam. Adam was created "from the dust of the earth" and therefore on the planet earth and not in a garden in heaven.

The Bible describes the physical location of the Garden.[5] Names of cities and rivers are mentioned to describe the location, and these include Assyria, and the rivers Tigris and Euphrates (both of which are still there today), as well as Pishon and Gihon.

There is indeed an Eden in heaven and this was where Lucifer (now called Satan) was created, and from where he was thrown down to the planet earth.[6] But the Eden where man was created is here on planet earth. The word 'Eden' simply means "garden of delight" or "garden of God." Whoever wrote the Qur'an must have mixed these things up somewhere.

What the Bible means by the "fall of man" (through

---

[3] Sura 2:36
[4] Genesis 1:26-30
[5] Genesis 2:7-15
[6] Ezekiel 28:12-19

Adam) is the spiritual separation of man from the glory of God:

> "For all (through Adam) have sinned, and come (fall) short of the glory of God."[7]

Man receives the nature of sin through this sin of Adam, and since God is completely holy, our sin separates us from Him. It is because of this basic misunderstanding of the fall of Adam and its implications on all his descendants that many Muslims find it difficult to understand the issue of salvation and redemption.

The Preserved Scriptures

We must bear in mind that many Jews were in Arabia at the time of Muhammad and had much influence on him. These Jews said their scriptures (especially the Torah) were preserved in the Ark (of the Covenant).[8] When Muhammad heard this, he thought the Ark must be in the presence of God in heaven, so he began to say that his own "scriptures" were from the "Mother of the Book" [umm al kitab] or "the Preserved Tablet" [*Al Lauh al-Mahfuz*] in heaven.[9] That was the origin of the "made-in-heaven" claim of the Qur'an.

The Jews and Christians who should have explained to him what they meant by their scriptures being preserved on tablets in the Ark of God did not. They ridiculed the man; but they paid for this with their lives. Muhammad saw them as dangerous to his mission and ordered their

---

[7] Romans 3:23
[8] Exodus 25:21; 1 Kings 8:9
[9] Suras 43:3-4 and 85:22

killing and expulsion from their settlements in Yathrib and the whole of the Arabian Peninsula.[10]

Historical Fallacies and Anachronisms

Sura 2:246-251 is a mix-up of the story of the children of Israel demanding a king, and the story of Gideon's victory as well as the killing of Goliath. How three separate historical events can be joined together in one event we do not understand.

The Man Haman

We are introduced to Sura 28 with these words:

"These are verses of the book that makes things clear."

With such introduction, we are called to expect a clear sequence of historical records. It continues:

"We recite you some of the news of Moses and Pharaoh in truth for a believing people…"

Then it talks of Pharaoh oppressing the children of Israel and how God wished to exalt them:

"And to establish them in the earth, and to show Pharaoh and Haman and their hosts that (very thing) against which they were fearing."

With our expectation of true history in this sura, we are shocked to see Haman mentioned together with Pharaoh. Verse 38 says that Pharaoh commanded Haman to build him a tower to reach heaven. Here, three different historical events and personalities are brought together in one scene. The tower is the Tower of Babel, built about 750

---

[10] Sura 5:51; Sura 9:29

years before the Pharaoh or Moses were born. Haman
was not in Egypt with any Pharaoh. He served in the palace of the King of Persia, Ahasuerus, about one thousand
one hundred years separated from the Pharaoh of Moses'
time. This mix-up is repeated in Sura 40:23-24.

Yusuf Ali, quite aware of this obvious historical blunder, attempts to explain it away as though only Muslims
would read his commentary:

> "Haman was evidently Pharaoh's minister, not to
> be confounded with a Haman who is mentioned
> in the Old Testament (Esther 3:1) as a minister of
> Ahasuerus (Xerxes), King of Persia, the same who
> invaded Greece and ruled from BC 485 to 464."[11]

This is a total confusion, and Ali is quite aware of the
weakness of his argument. In fact, technically, it is not
even an argument because there is no single premise in
his statements. He knows his explanation is lame, but
since he cannot accept this obvious error in his made-in-
heaven Qur'an, he must gallantly dismiss it.

Haman is known even in secular history, and therefore
Ali's defense of the Qur'an is untenable. He says, "Haman was evidently Pharaoh's minister..." Where is the
evidence? There is none in the Qur'an and none in his
commentary to prove the existence of such a Haman in
Pharaoh's time. By using the word "evidently," Ali is trying to psyche the unwary reader into believing that there
is evidence in that Qur'anic verse. We refuse to accept the
word "evidently" as a substitute for evidence.

---

11 Yusuf Ali, Commentary No. 4689.

Moreover, Ali rendered the word for "tower" as "palace" in his own translation. This he did deliberately to cover up the problem of this tower reaching heaven at the time of Moses and Pharaoh. Other translators like G. Sales, Palmer, Rodwell, Arberry, etc., translated it as "tower."

Mary and Miriam

Muhammad had a particular interest in Mary, the mother of Jesus. A whole sura is named after her (Sura 19). However, several things are muddled up concerning the history of Mary that an honest Muslim must re-examine and then ask himself whether indeed this Qur'an came from the hand of the omniscient God.

Apart from the mention that Mary was the mother of Jesus, and was a virgin when she conceived the Lord Jesus, everything else said about her in the Qur'an is false. Sura 66:12 refers to her as daughter of Imran (Amram, father of Moses). This is a tragedy to Islam. Muslim apologists like Yusuf Ali have made unsuccessful attempts to explain this away. The Bible says:

> "And the name of Amram's wife was Jochebed, the daughter of Levi, whom her mother bare to Levi in Egypt: and she bare unto Amram Aaron and Moses, and Miriam their sister."[12]

If the Qur'an says Mary, the mother of Jesus, is Miriam, the sister of Aaron, then Mary was a sister of Moses. But Moses, Aaron, and Miriam died about 1,500 years before Mary, the mother of Jesus, was born. In fact, there is no record of any child by Miriam, Aaron's sister. The

---

[12] Numbers 26:59

problem is that the Qur'an has mixed up the "Miriam" or "Mariam" of Aaron's time with the "Mary," the mother of Jesus, whose name can also be called "Mariam."

Who mixed these things up in the Qur'an: Allah or Muhammad? Can God make such a mistake? Our question then resounds: Who wrote the Qur'an? If this mistake was made by Muhammad, it is pardonable, since any human being can be wrong. But if Allah inspired him or gave him the Qur'an, then we have many questions.

A Muslim has the right to believe that the Qur'an was divinely authored or inspired, even at the expense of reason and in defiance of all evidence. As Christians, we do not force anybody to reject or believe anything, but we realize that where a man puts his faith determines his fate for eternity. We cannot head in a wrong direction and arrive at the right destination. We have the fundamental human right to continue in a lie with earnestness and go to hell. Or we can embrace the truth and enter into life eternal with God. The choice is open to every individual.

The Qur'an says Mary and Zacharias were together in the sanctuary when the "angels" came to Zacharias to give the prophecy about John. It also says that Zacharias was Mary's guardian and that Mary stayed in the sanctuary until she gave birth to Jesus Christ.

The truth, however, is that Zacharias had received the angelic message and his wife had already conceived (the prophecy fulfilled) six months before Mary heard of it.[13] Also, Mary and Zacharias did not live in the same town,

---

13 Luke 1:36

so Zacharias could not have been her guardian. It was AFTER the angel appeared to Mary in "a city of Galilee called Nazareth" that she visited Zacharias' house in Judah to spend three months with his wife, Elizabeth, who was Mary's relative.[14] Mary had already conceived before going to Zacharias' house. This is evident in Elizabeth's prophetic greeting to her when they met.[15] Mary was not at the place where Zacharias received his prophecy; nor was Zacharias at the place where Mary received her prophecy. Lastly, the angel visited Mary in a house, not a sanctuary.

According to the Qur'an, "angels called to him (Zacharias) as he stood praying in the sanctuary…" and the angels also appeared to Mary.

First, it was only one angel, Gabriel, who appeared to Zacharias, not "angels." It was the same Gabriel who appeared to Mary. The Qur'an says it was angels.[16] A contradiction comes up when Allah says:

> "…We sent to her Our *Ruh*[17] and he appeared before her in the form of a man in all respects."[18]

The Qur'an's story says Zacharias was mute for three days. The true story in the Bible says he was mute throughout his wife's pregnancy. He spoke only on the day the child was being named.[19] That must have been at least nine months of dumbness. Not three days!

---

[14] Luke 1:26, 39
[15] Luke 1:42-43
[16] Sura 3: 35-42
[17] The Arabic word here 'ruh' means 'spirit', but some translators translate it as 'angel.'
[18] Sura 19:17 (Al-Hilali)
[19] Luke 1:5-20

Actually, a number of these errors were copied from one Jewish book of fables called *The Protevangelion's James the Lesser*, written around 300 A.D. Jews and Christians knew the difference between their scriptures and their folktales. The author of the Qur'an, however, did not, which is one of the tragedies of the book. Jews never equate their fables with their scriptures.[20]

For example, scholars have identified much from the stories of Abraham in the Qur'an as taken from *Midrash Rabbah*, a Jewish book of legends, and not from Jewish Scriptures. The concept of "seven heavens and seven hells" as stated in Sura 15:44 and 17:44 came from a tradition called *Hagigah and Zuhal*. The two angels "Harut and Marut" mentioned in Sura 2:102 are two old idols worshipped in Armenia. 'Marut' is, actually, the Hindu god of wind. How these and several other items came from the 'original Qur'an in heaven, we do not know.

The Prophecy about John the Baptist

In the prophecy about the birth of John the Baptist, the Qur'an quotes the angel as saying to Zacharias:

> "'…Rejoice, Zakarias,' came the answer. 'You shall be given a son, and he shall be called Yahya: a name no man has borne before him.'"[21]

The Qur'an is wrong here when it says that nobody had borne the name "John" (Yahya) before this time. The Hebrew word for John is Johanan and it means "Jehovah has been gracious." There were at least *eleven* people who

---

[20] 2 Peter 1:16
[21] Sura 19:1-11

bore this name or a derivation of it in the Old Testament before John the Baptist was born.[22]

Prof. A. J. Arberry's translation says "...no namesake have We given him aforetime." Rodwell and Palmer both say "...that name we have given to none before him." George Sale says "...We have not caused any to bear the same name before him." The Bible says no man *in the family of Zacharias* had that name before. It does not say that nobody ever bore the name.

Yusuf Ali was aware of this problem and hid it by changing the meaning of the verse. His translation reads:

> "...His name shall be Yahya: on none by that name have we conferred distinction before."[23]

That lie did the trick!

The Qur'an says Zacharias was "invoking" Allah in a shrine when the angel appeared to him. The God of the Bible is not invoked or worshipped in a shrine. Evil spirits can be invoked through enchantments, incense, and incantations. No man can invoke God to appear by any means. If God comes down anywhere, it is at His volition, and sometimes in response to praise or worship, but not by invocation.

Ishmael or Isaac?

Apart from the distorted history we have seen in the Qur'an, many Muslim leaders ignore the Qur'an to establish their own doctrine. For example, which son did God

---

[22] Jeremiah 40:9-10; 12:4,12-14; 2 Chronicles 28:12; Ezra 8:12; Nehemiah 6:18; Ezra 10:6; Nehemiah 12:22
[23] Yusuf Ali, Commentary. No. 3331.

promise Abraham in his old age, Ishmael or Isaac? The
Qur'an says Ishaq (Isaac).[24] The Islamic world believes it
was Ishmael. Both cannot be right.

Which son did God ask Abraham to sacrifice to Him?
The answer is: the son that was promised. Which son was
this? The story is found in Suras 11, 15 and 37. Sura 11
says:

> "Our messengers came to Ibrahim with good news.
> They said: 'Peace!' 'Peace!' he said, and hastened to
> bring them a roasted calf. But when he saw that
> their hands did not reach to it, he was afraid of
> them: (but) they said: 'Do not be alarmed. We are
> sent forth to the people of Lut.'

> "His wife, who was waiting on them, rejoiced. We
> gave her the good news of Ishaq, and after Ishaq
> of Yaqub.

> "'Alas!' she replied. 'How shall I bear a child when I
> am old and my husband is well-advanced in years?
> This is indeed a strange thing.'"[25]

Pickthall's translation of verses 71-72 says:

> "'And his wife, standing by, laughed when We gave
> her good tidings (of the birth) of Isaac, and, after
> Isaac, of Jacob. She said: 'Oh, woe is me! Shall I
> bear a child when I am an old woman, and this
> my husband is an old man? Lo! This is a strange
> thing!'

---

[24] Sura 11:69-73; 15:51-53
[25] Sura 11:69-72 (Mahmud Y. Zayid)

Sura 37 gives the occasion where Abraham had earlier prayed for the son:

"100. O my Lord! Grant me a righteous (son)!

"101. So We (Allah) gave him the good news of a boy ready to suffer and forbear.

"102. Then when (the son) reached (the age of) (serious) work with him, he said: 'O my son! I see in vision that I offer thee in sacrifice. Now see what is thy view!' (The son) said, 'O my father! Do as thou art commanded. Thou will find me if Allah so wills one practicing Patience and Constancy!'

"103. So when they had both submitted their wills (to Allah) and he had laid down prostrate on his forehead (for sacrifice),

"104. We called out to him, 'O Abraham!

"105. Thou hast already fulfilled the vision' -- Thus indeed do We reward those who do right.

"106. For this was obviously a trial -

"107. And We ransomed him with a momentous sacrifice.

"108. And We left (this blessing) for him among generations (to come) in later times.

"109. Peace and salutation to Abraham!"

In Sura 37, the righteous son that Abraham asked God for is not mentioned by name. But the son is mentioned clearly in Sura 11:71.

The Qur'an says it was "the righteous son" that Abraham asked for, the son God promised He would give, that

God later ordered him to sacrifice. The name of the son is given as Ishaq (Isaac). Yet, many Arabs believe that the son God promised and later asked Abraham to sacrifice is Ishmael. They do not care what the Qur'an says.

This lie is repeated all over the world every year during the Islamic festival to commemorate this sacrifice.

7

Final Authority: Bible or Qur'an?

We have read several books written by Muslims undermining the authority of the Bible as the Word of God. On the other hand, Muslims are always morbidly afraid of any non-Muslim commenting on the Qur'an.

Countless books have been written ABOUT the Bible, either by believers of the Book or by its enemies. In the providence of God, the printing press with movable type was invented at a time when there was a critical need for the circulation of the scriptures to counter heresies and spread the gospel. It reserves the honor of being the first book to come off that press. Despite all attempts by kings of the earth and many religious leaders to destroy the Book, pervert its message, or prevent its distribution, it remains the best seller of all ages.

As a lost sinner, I wondered at its probe into my sinful nature. As a believer now, I rejoice at the peace, comfort and assurance of salvation I have in it. As a student, I marvel at the sublimity of the Book, its historicity, its scientific base, and the authority of its tone. In it I see the only hope for a world leading itself to destruction.

It is impossible to fully know the world history or understand the events in the international scene today without knowing the Bible. Its prophetic authority makes it more relevant than tomorrow's newspapers. The Bible will continue to baffle the ignorant "learned" heathen until they humble themselves at the feet of the Lord to discover the truth and the life in the Word.

Having rejected the Word of life, man runs about in delusion and depravity of mind seeking help in yoga, horoscopes and all kinds of New Age religions, even though he pretends he does not believe in the supernatural.

The Bible was written by more than forty different writers from all walks of life — kings (David), princes (Moses), priests (Ezekiel, Jeremiah), prophets, politicians and scholars (Ezra, Isaiah, Daniel, Paul, etc.), soldiers (Joshua), fishermen (Peter, John), herdsmen (Amos), civil servants (Matthew), etc.

Most of these people lived many years apart, most never having met each other. Yet the thematic harmony of the whole Book runs from Genesis through Revelation. The writers wrote the same message, yet not one wrote the same way or the same thing. One book finds its complement in the other until there is a consummation of all things in the book of Revelation. Even the Tree of Life forfeited in Genesis is regained in Revelation.

We regard it as a book guarded by one Intelligent Mind,

the Mind of the Spirit of a faithful and consistent God. Most of those who accused the Bible of being unscientific and contradictory have begun to swallow their words as they are discovering their own intellectual emptiness (despite their academic titles) and their ignorance of the diction and interpretation of the Scripture. Only the uninformed still talk of a lack in scientific basis or historical fact in the Bible.

The Bible was written by several people and yet has a consistent theme. The Qur'an, on the other hand, was supposedly written by one man, or as Muslims want us to believe, was written in heaven by Allah, yet it surprises us with so many serious categorical contradictions.

It is necessary to dig up one or two such contradictions here to aid our understanding of who might be speaking in the book.

Remember, many Muslims say Muhammad was illiterate. The Qur'an describes him as "al-nabi al-ummi," (the unlearned or unlettered prophet.)[1] Although some scholars have disputed the meaning of this verse, and the modern translators of the Qur'an in European languages try to avoid this meaning,[2] such a claim and interpretation by Muslims in Islamic lands is necessary to validate the assertion that the Qur'an was not written by Muhammad but came down hot from heaven and was given to the man. And since it is directly from heaven, it is therefore free from human instrumentality.

---

[1] Sura 7:158

[2] The present Dutch translation of the Qur'an made by the Ahmadiyya sect renders this expression as "the pure Prophet."

The cosmogonical and cosmological[3] data in the Qur'an is in a flux. According to Sura 54:50, the whole Creation was done in the twinkle of an eye. That is, when God spoke his Word of creation, the whole universe came into existence immediately in a split second, that is, in less than one day. Yet Sura 41:9 says the world was created in two days. Verse 10 of the same sura says it took four days. Verse 12 says "seven heavens" were created in two days. But then Suras 7:54; 10:3; and 32:4 say the Creation was done in six days. Presumably by the time he received the "six-day creation" revelation, Muhammad had already heard of the true Biblical account in Genesis. He probably forgot to withdraw and destroy the former written "revelations."

So during the compilation of the Qur'an after his death, everything was bound together by his followers. Sura 32:5 also says a day is actually "a thousand years of your reckoning," thereby compounding our confusion. In Sura 70:4, we read that a day with Allah is not 1,000 years as we have read in Sura 32, but 50,000 years!

We will examine more of these contradictions in the next chapter. Here, however, we need to take one or two more. These have to do with statements about Christianity. It is interesting to note that with all the animosity towards everything Christian, there are still places in the Qur'an with some revealing truths. Allah is quoted, for instance, as saying that the followers of Jesus Christ shall be exalted above all others until the Day of resurrection

---

[3] That is, beliefs about the creation and development of the universe.

(Sura 3:55). [4] Again, the Qur'an talks of the Bible as the "guide for the wise."[5] It confirms Jesus' virgin birth, and that He was the Word of God, and the Spirit of God who put on the flesh of man, etc. One of such verses says:

> "And the woman that kept her virginity, we breathed into her Our Spirit, and we made her and her Son, a sign for all mankind."[6]

If such basic truths are in the Qur'an and were revealed by Allah, why then do many Christians not regard the book as a holy book of God? Our answer is that because there are categorical denials of all these truths in the same book, and we believe that a holy book should be consistent, especially when it comes to matters affecting the salvation of man.

For another example, Allah is quoted as saying to Jesus:

> "Surely, I will allow you (or cause you to DIE), and raise thee to Myself..."[7]

Again, in Sura 19:33, Jesus is quoted as saying:

> "And the peace of God was on me on the day that I was born; and it shall be on me on the day that I would DIE, and the day I would be raised up to life." (emphasis mine.)

Compare this with Sura 19:15, where the same thing is said of John the Baptist. They know John died.

---

[4] It is interesting that Dr. Al-Hilali and Muhsin Khan had to insert 47 personal words into this verse in order to pervert the clear meaning!

[5] Sura 5:48 (Ali); 5:44 (Al-Hilali)

[6] Sura 21:91 (Al-Hilali *et. al.* perverted this verse by their insertions).

[7] Sura 3:55

However, in an attempt to explain away the crucifixion of Jesus, Muhammad says later that Jesus did not die, and was not nailed on the cross. Rather, "it only seemeth so in their eyes."[8]

Here is a person whom Muslims say was illiterate telling us that an event that happened over five hundred years before he was born "only seemeth so."

How could the historical event of the crucifixion of Jesus be denied? There are only two possibilities. I think Muhammad believed Jesus was too powerful to have been killed by wicked people. He regarded Jesus as a great prophet who raised the dead, opened the eyes of the blind, and healed the sick. How could such a person have fallen 'helplessly into the hands of His enemies, and been abandoned by God?' That was probably his thinking.

It may also be that Muhammad deliberately denied the death and resurrection of Jesus because it would have serious implications on his other messages. Moreover, it would have proven that Jesus had power over death and therefore was qualified to be the Saviour.

Most Islamic scholars don't know what to believe in the Qur'an concerning the death and resurrection of Jesus Christ. Yusuf Ali is confused, but he is honest in his reasoning on the issue:

> "Christ was not crucified (IV: 157). But those who believe that he never died should ponder over this verse, (that is Verse 33 of Sura 19)."[9]

---

[8] Sura 158–4:157
[9] Commentary No. 2485.

Here, Ali implies that Jesus died, but was not crucified. He did not explain. How, where did Jesus die? What happened to Him at the end of His ministry on earth? He did not explain because the Qur'an is ambiguous about it. The issue is therefore left to the fertile imaginations of different Muslim sects.

In a bid to explain these conflicting verses and to deliberately ignore the need for a shedding of blood to save mankind, different Muslim sects have developed different ideas. The Ahmadiyyah sect, holding on the theory of Venturini, says Jesus only fainted on the cross or at most was only half dead, and that He regained His consciousness while in the grave and then ran away secretly to India where He lived and died a normal death at a good old age.

This is the view held by the popular South African Muslim pamphleteer, Ahmed Deedat, in some of his pamphlets titled *Resurrection or Resuscitation?*, *Crucifixion or Crucifiction?*, etc.[10]

Some other commentators brought in the idea of machine-god (deux-ex-machina), which is a dramatic device whereby a supernatural intervention is introduced to avert an inevitable but unnecessary tragedy at the end of a play. According to the Muslims who hold this view, God circumvented the crucifixion of Jesus by miraculously removing Him from the cross to heaven in the twinkle of an eye and replacing Him with someone God made to

---

[10] John Gilchrist has written replies to Deedat's pamphlets. Contact: Jesus to the Muslims, 4b Bright Street, Benoni, 1500 South Africa. Or see his answers online at: www.answering-islam.org/gilchrist.

look exactly like Jesus, and who was eventually crucified in His stead.

Who was this substitute? Opinions also differ on this. The popular consensus is Judas Iscariot. Therefore, it wasn't Jesus the soldiers crucified: "It only seemeth so in their eyes."

This "catching away" theory was formulated by Muslims in the Middle Ages and is clearly entrenched in Chapter 112, verses 13-17 of the so-called gospel of Barnabas, written at that time by a former Roman Catholic turned Muslim.

This book is popular and highly venerated among Muslims as a good weapon for opposing Christian teachings about Jesus. It is therefore not surprising that Muslims publish this book (especially in Pakistan) and circulate it only in their midst. This fake gospel quotes Jesus as saying to Barnabas:

> "Know therefore Barnabas, that for this I have to be wary. One of my disciples will betray me for thirty pieces of silver. Furthermore, I am sure that he who betray me will be killed in my name, because God will lift me up from the earth and change the appearance of the one who betrays me so that everyone will think him to be me. And when he dies a very awful death, I will remain in that shame a long time in the world. But when Muhammad, the holy apostle of God, comes, this disgrace will be removed from me.[11]

---

[11] Chapter 17-112:13

It is strange that intelligent Muslims would leave the true story of the Gospel of Christ in the Bible and cling to such a crude forgery. This book even has excerpts from the poem of Dante!

Our Muslim friends need to understand that the cross of Christ is not a tragedy. It is a victory over the devil and sin. The devil himself knows this. He can never forget what happened early on that resurrection morning. During this period, Jesus:

> "...having spoiled principalities and powers, he made a shew of them openly, triumphing over them..."[12]

The cross was God's formula of "life through death." Jesus did not come to establish a worship system. He did not come to give a law but to give His love. His law was love.

He came primarily to die, and there was no need for Him to escape it.[13] If God did not want Jesus to be killed, there would have been no need to "steal" Him away. All He would have had to have done was send down a few angels to destroy the soldiers and allow Jesus to continue His ministry there in Jerusalem.[14] "Stealing Jesus" away would mean showing God's helplessness and defeat by terminating the ministry of Christ prematurely.

Some want us to believe that Jesus was a nice gentleman who preached love and peace, then events got out

---

[12] Colossians 2:15
[13] Matthew 16:21
[14] Jesus Himself hinted at this possibility in Matthew 26:53.

of hand and he fell helplessly into the hands of an angry mob.

That is not true. Jesus went to the cross willingly. He was in absolute control of every event in His life, including the timing! Even on the night of His arrest when Judas, who was to identify Him, was still delaying going to the chief priests for the deal, the Lord had to hasten him: "That thou doest, do quickly."[15] That is, "What you are about to do, do it quickly. Don't waste my time." This shows that His arrest had to take place that particular night unfailingly, according to His strict timetable. It also shows that there was a will in Him to die, and it was never rescinded.

If Muslims maintain that Jesus never died but was taken up to heaven alive, then they must admit these logical conclusions: Jesus is still alive today just as He was on earth, for we cannot imagine Him dying in heaven. Secondly, the claim of Muslims that Muhammad is the successor of Jesus is null and void if Jesus has not died (and never will).

Some other Muslim exegetes say the Qur'an verses are rather predictions of Jesus' death when He returns to the earth.[16] If that is the case, then we would say that until Jesus returns, nobody can succeed Him.

The person Muslims say Muhammad was succeeding is still alive. But Muhammad himself is dead. If it was the physical absence of Jesus on earth that made Muhammad

---

[15] John 13:27
[16] Sura 3:55 and 19:33

a "natural successor," what happens now that Muhammad is no longer here? Who owns the throne?

The fact is that the throne has never been vacant because the King is still alive. Even genuine prophets of the real God have come and gone forever. The Bible says death prevented them from continuing in office; but because Jesus lives forever, He has a permanent priesthood. Therefore, He is able to save all those who come to God through Him, because He always lives to intercede for them:

> "And they truly were many priests, because they were not suffered (allowed) to continue by reason of death: But this man (Jesus), because he continueth ever, hath an unchangeable priesthood. Wherefore, he is able also to save them to the uttermost that come unto God by him, seeing he ever liveth to make intercession for them."[17]

He intercedes for us. On the other hand, Muslims have to pray and intercede for Muhammad for peace. Any time they mention his name, a Muslim must say, "May the peace of Allah be upon him." Christians do not pray for Jesus. He is more than our prayers. We don't say "peace be upon him." He is our peace. He said, "My peace I give unto you..."[18] Yes, He has peace to offer. In fact, when Muslims call His name, they say, 'He upon whom peace rests'. Sura 19:33 says peace was upon Jesus from the very day He was born.

---

[17] Hebrews 7:23-25
[18] John 14:27

Where is Muhammad today? If he is in paradise, should he not be in peace? If so, why should we pray for peace for him? If he is not in peace, can our prayers help him? Should we pray for our prophet? Should not he pray for us? These are questions I ask Muslims to think about.

Jesus died and was resurrected on the third day. He ascended into heaven. From there he will descend physically to rule and judge the earth. Muslim leaders really hate the idea of the resurrection of Jesus. That is why it has become necessary for them to deny His death first. It is amazing how much effort they have put into twisting the translation of these verses to hide the meaning.

In Sura 3:55, Muhammad Marmaduke Pickthall translated the expression rendered "I will cause you to die" as "I am gathering thee…" Going to the original Arabic Qur'an, the expression here is *Inni muta-waf-feeka.* Sincere Arabs must ask themselves why Pickthall translated this as "gathering." Dr. Anis Shorrosh said:

> "As an Arab, I have never known of any other meaning than death for this expression, within or without the Qur'an"[19]

We can understand the reason for Pickthall's translation. The Australian Anti-Communist Crusader, Dr Fred Swartz, has observed that:

> "No matter how clear the evidence is, people can always find an interpretation that will allow them to cling to what they want to believe."

[19] Shorrosh, A., *Islam Revealed: A Christian Arab's View of Islam,* (Nashville: Thomas Nelson, 1989) p. 97.

The fact is that the doctrine of the cross and the consequent resurrection is offensive to Muslims and they must explain it away.

Commenting on Sura 3:59, Yusuf Ali says:

> "Jesus was as dust just as Adam was or humanity is."[20]

Ali only echoes what the Qur'an says in that verse. Christians take this view as blasphemous because we know Jesus is divine. God indeed cursed Adam and humanity to return to dust from which man was created:

> "…for dust thou art, and unto dust shalt thou return."[21]

Adam died and his body returned to the dust after decaying. All humanity is under this curse of putrefaction. Even if a dead body is mummified, the fact that a body has no life makes it no more important than the dust. The body is no longer a "he" but an "it," and no less an "it" than the dust! So what if cremated? It is even worse to turn to ashes than to dust!

Even though Muhammad said he was an ordinary man, and though Muslims claim they do not worship him, it is evident the man has been exalted to the level of deity. That is why Muslims often talk of "blaspheming our prophet." They do not realize that they commit the Islamic unforgivable sin of *shirk* by regarding Muhammad as one who can be blasphemed. Only God is divine, and

---

[20] Yusuf Ali, *Qur'an: Text, Translation and Commentary,* Commentary No. 398.
[21] Genesis 3:19

therefore the only One that can be blasphemed! Jesus, as the Son of God, can be blasphemed, and the Holy Spirit of God can be blasphemed because they are God.[22] Many Muslims have done this consistently through their writings and preaching which are taken from the Qur'an itself. As an ordinary human being like us all, Muhammad was also under this curse of dust-to-dust put on mankind as said above. The dust and the dry bones in his grave in Medina today are proof of this.

Where is the body of Jesus, whom Muslims believe was "as dust just as Adam or humanity"? Where is that dust? Even though many Muslims deny that Jesus died or was resurrected, they all agree, according to their Qur'an, that Christ was taken up to heaven, body, soul and spirit. Since He cannot die up there, they must conclude that He is still alive today in regal glory, waiting for His second coming. It necessarily follows that He is "the same yesterday, and to day, and for ever!"[23]

Now if the body of Jesus defied the curse put on humanity, does this not raise Him above humanity? It is, indeed, because Jesus was human, yet above humanity, that He is qualified to be the Saviour of the world.

A story has it that when Muhammad died, his people thought that having proclaimed himself "the Seal of the Prophets," and therefore the greatest, he would at least rise up, probably on the third day and ascend to heaven bodily as Jesus did. For this reason, they refused to dig his grave deep; neither did they bury the remains in a closed

---

[22] Acts 5:3-4, John 14:7; John 20:28
[23] Hebrew 13:8

coffin, because they wanted to make it easier for him to come out of the grave.

But Death and the Grave held him and have never released him. If that story is true, we do not think Muslims should be disappointed that the remains of their prophet decayed and became dust. Allah never promised Muhammad would resurrect like Jesus; so why should they feel disappointed?

However, everything that Muhammad did, and the things that were done to him by his disciples, as recorded in the Traditions, must be copied as examples to follow. So even today, Muslims do not dig the ground deep to bury their dead; neither do they normally bury in a coffin. And they must bury the dead within twenty four hours. Many of them, though, do not know how these traditions began.

False messiahs may rise and make bogus claims about themselves. But death always comes and deals its blow to them and they are consumed in the earth. The Eternal King of kings, some sixty years after His resurrection and Ascension, spoke to John:

> "I am He that liveth, and was dead; and, behold, I am alive for evermore, Amen; and have the keys of hell and of death."[24]

Muslims need to understand that the cross of Jesus was necessary. "The wages of sin is DEATH"[25] and because Jesus was carrying the sin of the whole world at the

---

[24] Revelation 1:18
[25] Romans 6:23

moment He was on the cross, He had to DIE! By that, God made "His soul an offering for sin…"[26] But to give His believers victory over sin, as well as over Satan, demons and the second death, Jesus had to rise from the dead. Many enemies of the gospel today deny these facts, but none have been able to refute them. All their "proofs" only prove how uninformed they are concerning these historical events.

About fifty days after the death and resurrection of Christ, Peter stood in the midst of several thousand Jews in Jerusalem on the day of Pentecost and spoke about what Christ's death and the resurrection had done for mankind. No single listener rose to say that Jesus was not crucified. They all knew that this was the talk of the town.

Muhammad was born over 500 years later to say that Jesus Christ did not die, and that it was Allah who told him so.

As Christians, we reject the Qur'an because it denies history—history recorded not only by Christians but by many secular writers who lived during the time of the early Christians. They could have denied the Christians' claims if they were untrue. Yes, the Qur'an has certain truths, but many intelligent people reject the book as divine because they know that a half-truth is more dangerous than a blatant lie.

The devil is a liar and the inspirer of all lies. Jesus said that when Satan lies, he is not doing anything strange, but:

---

[26] Isaiah 53:10, 6-12; 2 Corinthians 5:21

"When he speaketh a lie, he speaketh of his own:
for he is a liar, and the father of it."[27]

It must be realized, however, that Satan is not just a liar but a deceiver! And to be an excellent deceiver, he knows he has to add one or two facts into a bundle of lies. That is how he deceives many people today in false religions and cults. They use some statements in the Bible to establish their cults and destroy themselves.

Therefore, the fact that there are a few biblically true statements in the Qur'an does not make the book the Word of God. It is a classic diabolical deception. As Tennyson the poet wrote:

"A lie that's a half-truth

is the wickedest lie of all,

For a lie that's all a lie

can be met with and fought outright

But a lie that is a half-truth

is a harder matter to fight."

On the other hand, the presence of some of these facts in the Qur'an serves as a testimony against all Muslims who reject the gospel of Jesus Christ. We thank God that some of these bits of truths have led some Muslims to inquire more of Christ in the Bible and they have thereby found Him as He really is.[28]

In his book, *Buddha, Muhammad and Christ*, Dr.

---

[27] John 8:44

[28] You may ask for the author's *How We Found Jesus: 20 Ex-Muslims Testify.* (firelineinternational@yahoo.co.uk).

Marcus Dodds observes that Muhammad's book can never be taken by serious-minded people as a reliable authority on the gospel of Jesus or as a history book on the heroes of the Bible:

> "His (Muhammad's) knowledge of Christianity is so meager and confused, that it is difficult to understand how even the most illiterate and mystified sectary fed on apocryphal gospels could have conveyed to him such notions of the gospel. Of the great enlightening history of Israel, as a history, he knows nothing and has merely caught up some childish tales from the Talmud and some garbled legends of the Hebrew patriarchs and great men."[29]

In his own evaluation of the Qur'an, Thomas Carlyle (1795-1881), in his controversial work, *On Heroes and Hero Worship*, complains that the Qur'an is nothing but "a wearisome, long-winded entanglement; most crude and recondite; insupportable stupidity, in short."

Someone may ask: if this be so, why then do millions of people, including respectable and learned men, believe in the Qur'an as a holy book of God, and why are many ready to kill or be killed in order to defend it?

There are many reasons for this. Naturally, man prefers a religion that is in consonance with his wicked nature. He prefers a religion that appeals to the worst in him, approves of charms and violence, and makes him feel truly pious.

---

[29] *Buddha, Muhammad and Christ*, Dr Marcus Dodds, pp. 13-14.

Moreover, there is an inherent power in repetition. For example, when an obvious lie is repeated over and over, it eventually becomes convincing and believable. That is the psychology of advertising. The Russian psychologist, Pavlov, knew this, and his theory became the basis for the science of brainwashing effectively used by the Communist world.

It is a system being explored very well in Islam, and it works. A Muslim has been made to repeat certain things so often that it has become impossible to imagine the error of such statements. And he is ready to arrest, jail or even slay people to defend these "truths."

The power of repetition has been used to make even non-Muslims accept the claim that the Qur'an is elegant, wonderful and non-comparable and that Islam is a religion of peace. Careful students have refused to be carried away by such cheap appraisals.

We have also discovered that a person can teach anything and get some followers, especially if he is consistent. That is why every philosopher, cultist, and terrorist will always have disciples, no matter how strict his terms may be.

Above all these is the fact that all lies are spiritual. This is because Satan, the father of all lies, is a spirit. That is why it takes spiritual warfare to fight a lie. In the words of Thackeray, one would adduce concerning people's veneration of some of these "holy books" that:

"A lie once set going, having the breath of life breathed into it by the father of lying, and ordered

to run its diabolical little course, lives with a pro-
digious vitality."[30]

Yes, a lie may continue to live but the deceived victims
have the will-power to get themselves out of it. This is
made easier by the power of the gospel of Christ. If this
book succeeds in getting the reader out of a popular deception, it has achieved its sole purpose.

"A lie should be trampled upon and extinguished
wherever found. I am for fumigating the atmo-
sphere, where I suspect falsehood, like pestilence,
breathes around me." - Thomas Carlyle.

---

[30] From "On a Hundred Years Hence" in *Roundabout Papers*, by
William Makepeace Thackeray (1811-1863).

8

Contradictions in the Qur'an

MUSLIMS cannot conceive the possibility of contradictions in the Qur'an. One proof they present to establish the divine inspiration of the Qur'an is the absence of contradictions.

The Qur'an itself says:

> "Do they not consider the Qur'an carefully? Had it been from other than Allah, they would surely have found therein many a contradiction."[1]

Therefore, proving contradictions in the Qur'an would be enough to settle the claim of divine inspiration. We have already examined a few of these in the previous chapter. Here we will see a few more.

On Forgiveness

Worshipping any other being than Allah is called *shirk*.

---

[1] Sura 4:82 (Al-Hilali)

It is an unforgivable sin in Islam.[2] Yet Sura 39:53 says Allah forgives ALL sins. Abraham committed this unforgivable sin in the Qur'an, and yet he is held as the father of Islam.[3] All angels (except Satan) committed this sin by worshipping Adam, apart from God only. That was when Allah is said to have commanded all angels to bow down and worship Adam on the day he was created.[4]

How could Allah command Iblis (Satan) and all angels to bow down in worship to a human being if it is an unforgivable sin to worship any being other than Allah? Moreover, if Satan is the only one who did not commit *shirk*, does that then imply that Satan is a Muslim?

Immutability and Abrogation of Allah's Word

In the Qur'an, we are told that Allah's words can be changed, substituted or abrogated.[5] However, we are also told that the words of Allah are immutable.[6]

The True Religion

Sura 22:17 says Muslims, Jews, Christians and Sabaens (or Sabians) will be rewarded in paradise because they believe in God and the last day, and do good. In other words, we do not all have to become Muslims to go to paradise. However Sura 3:85 says:

> "Whoso desireth other than Islam as a religion, it shall never therefore be accepted from him, and in the next world he shall be among the lost."

---

[2] Sura 4:48.

[3] Sura 6:76-78

[4] Sura 18:50; 7:11ff; 15:29-35

[5] Suras 17:86; 2:106; and 16:101

[6] Sura 6:34, 114; 10:64; 18:27

Sabeans were ancient settlers in South West Arabia at the time of Muhammad, who worshipped the sun, the moon and the stars. The Qur'an says these star and moon worshippers will go to heaven together with Muslims, Jews and Christians. So how can Muslims say that the reverence of the moon and the star is un-Islamic? What role does the moon play in Islam? How is that linked with the origin of the religion? Why is the symbol of the moon and the star on all mosques and Islamic flags?

Who or What is the Holy Spirit?

Neither Muhammad nor any Muslim is sure who the Holy Spirit is. Because of the references made to the 'Spirit' in the Qur'an regarding the conception of Jesus, some Muslim translators put 'Angel' in brackets when this 'Spirit' is mentioned. So they say it is Angel Gabriel. Some say it is God's breath released into Mary to become Jesus. Allah says in Sura 17:85:

> "And they ask you (O Muhammad) concerning the Ruh (the Spirit); say: "The Ruh (the Spirit) is one of the things, the knowledge of which is only with my Lord. And of knowledge, you (mankind) have been given only a little."

Since the Qur'an confesses here that it does not know what the Holy spirit is, we wish to explain: the Holy Spirit of God is God the Spirit, and not an angel. When Mary was to conceive, the Angel Gabriel who appeared to her said:

> "The Holy Ghost shall come upon thee, and the power of the Highest shall overshadow thee:

therefore also that holy thing which shall be born
of thee shall be called the Son of God."[7]

Here Gabriel was clearly differentiating himself from
the Holy Spirit that would come on Mary.

Who Was the First Muslim?

When Islam fully developed, Muhammad said Islam
started from the creation of man, so Adam was the first
Muslim. However, Sura 6:14, 163 says that Muhammad
was the first to surrender to Allah and become a Muslim.
Yet Sura 7:143 says Moses was the first Muslim.

On Cosmological Data

How many days did it take God to create the world?
As we noted in the previous chapter, Sura 41:9 says two
days. Verse 10 of the same sura says four days. Suras 32:4;
7:54, 103, and 10:3 say six days. Some Muslims try to
add 4 and 2 to say 4, 2, and 6 are the same. Of course, the
Qur'an does not say that, and we reject such reconcilia-
tory arithmetic.

Other Muslim commentators have explanations that
are even more confusing than the contradictions themselves. Yusuf A. Ali was perplexed, but with boldness, he
suggested his own views. In his commentary on Sura 41:9,
Ali wrote:

> "This is a difficult passage, describing the primal
> creation of our physical earth and the physical
> heavens around us. If we count the two days men-
> tioned in this verse, the four days in verse 10, and

---

[7] Luke 1:35

the two days mentioned in verse 12, we get a total of eight days, while in many passages the creation is stated to have taken place in six days: see vii.54, no.1031 and xxxii.4, n. 3632. The commentators understand the 'four Days' in verse 10 to include the two days in verse 9, so that the total for the universe comes to six days. This is reasonable, because the processes described in verse 9 and 10 form really one series. In the one case it is the creation of the formless matter of the earth; in the other case it is the gradual evolution of the form of the earth, its mountains and seas, and its animal and vegetable life..."[8]

We appreciate Ali's statement that Sura 41:9-12 is "a difficult passage." But that is an understatement. Better words would be "confusing" or "perplexing" or "embarrassing."

Sura 22:47 and 32:5 tell us that one day to Allah actually means 1,000 years, but Sura 70:4 says a day with Allah is 50,000 years. No, these passages are not difficult; they are clear; they just say conflicting things. In fact, Ali's commentary on this is even more "difficult" and confusing than the passages themselves. He compounds the issue by bringing in the theory of evolution. A full explanation of that theory destroys the whole foundation of the Qur'an.[9]

---

[8] Yusuf Ali, Commentary No. 4470.
[9] See the author's mini-book titled *The Academic Superstition Called Evolution*, published by Fireliners International. For more information, email: firelineinternational@yahoo.co.uk.

But with this confusion, Muslims can comfort themselves by going to Sura 3:7. It says that there are certain passages in the Qur'an that no human being can understand:

> He it is who has sent down to thee the Book (Qur'an). In it are verses basic or fundamental clear (in meaning); they are the foundations of the Book: others are not entirely clear. But those in whose hearts is perversity (depravity) follow the part thereof that is not entirely clear seeking discord and searching for its interpretation, but no one knows its true meaning except Allah."

The implication is that only people of perverse minds desire to fully understand the Qur'an! The pious should only memorize. To research into the Qur'an is to seek discord. So if we want peace, we must remain in ignorance.

In other words, only Allah can understand what he wrote. The problem is: if no human being can understand certain areas in the Qur'an, why were they written, and for whom?

Moreover, we have read earlier where Allah says:

> "O ye who believe! Ask not questions about things which, if made plain to you, may cause you trouble..."[10]

The Nature of the Problem

Muhammad received many "revelations" concerning creation. Later, he learned from the Jews and Christians

---

[10] Sura 5:101

that creation took six days. That is why we find this "six-day creation" more pronounced in his later revelations. In an attempt to preserve the sanctity of the earlier verses purportedly received from heaven, Muhammad did not destroy all the earlier statements written down as revelations. Or it could be that he forgot such contradictory accounts existed.

At his death (which was sudden), his devotees gathered every bit of material they could see in his house, plus some other Qur'an-related materials in other people's possession, and also wrote down what some who could recite were able to recollect, and bound them all together as "the Holy Qur'an."

When the modern Muslim studies the Qur'an, he is confronted with these various contradictions and illogical statements. But he pretends he does not see them, and deliberately glosses over them. A Muslim student who desires the truth would attempt a further quest, but must be ready to face attacks from other Muslims who must defend the Qur'an as made-in-heaven.

Sin and Judgment

In Sura 8:29, Allah promises to grant man an opportunity to judge between right and wrong. Yet in several other verses, the Qur'an says that man has no choice in making decisions for righteousness, even if he knows what is wrong; it is Allah himself who wills a man to do both good and evil.[11] The Qur'an teaches that going to heaven is determined by weighing one's works on a scale or balance

---

[11] Sura 74:31; 14:4; 16:37

(Sura 7:8-9). Yet, we read often, "Allah forgiveth whoever he wills." If forgiveness is his prerogative, of what use then is the scale of measuring one's goodness?

Although Allah says he forgives whoever he wills, he also says that it is never his will, his plan, or part of his program, to guide anybody and lead him or her to heaven:

> "If We *(Allah)* had so willed, We could certainly have brought every soul to its true guidance: But the Word from Me will come true, 'I will fill hell with jinns and men all together.'"[12]

We wish to ask: if many people and spirits were created purposely for hell, why do Muslims go about proselytizing? Why do they want world domination? If everybody becomes a Muslim, are they not changing the will and divine plan of Allah? Even the Qur'an says:

> "If it had been thy Lord's will, they would all have believed, - all who are on earth! Wilt thou then compel mankind, against their will to believe?"[13]

This admonition contradicts several other areas in the same Qur'an, quoting Allah as commanding Muhammad to compel non-Muslims to be converted or be killed or have their property confiscated or be forced to pay *jizya* (heavy taxes imposed on non-muslims in an Islamic country).[14]

Does a Muslim have any assurance in the Qur'an or in

---

[12] Sura 32:13 (Ali). See also Sura 7:178-180 (Al-Hilali).
[13] Sura 10:99
[14] See Sura 9:29, 41, 123; Sura 47:4, 8; 2:190-191

the Hadith that he is not one of those whom Allah has destined for hell? No. Everybody is just trying his best. Did Muhammad himself have such assurance? Let the Hadith speak:

> "I heard the Messenger of Allah say, 'Verily the Almighty and Glorious Allah caught one party (or sect in Islam) with His right hand and another with another hand, and said: 'This is for this, and this is for this, and I don't care.' I don't know which of the two parties I am.'"[15]

This passage refers to the day of the judgment of Allah when he will separate mankind into two parties and herd some to hell and some to paradise. Muhammad says that even he does not know to which party or side he belongs.

Who is to blame? A servant of the Lord has this to say:

> "We should like to suggest that God is consistent, righteous and holy. In the case of contradictions or any flaws of any kind in any record supposed to have come from Him, man must be blamed, and not God. It is intolerable to cover these up to protect the image of a book or prophet or possibly a religion and its leaders."[16]

---

[15] Mishkat ul Masabih, Vol. 3, ch. 32:32

[16] Nehls, Gerhard, *Destination Unknown*, (Nairobi: Life Challenge, Africa, P.O. Box 30127, Nairobi, Kenya) p. 7.

9

Salvation in the Qur'an

The word "salvation"[1] is a rare word in Islam. It appears clearly only three times in the entire Qur'an.[2] Yet it is supposed to be a book from heaven; a book about salvation for mankind.

The whole Bible is about the salvation of man. It follows chronologically from the beginning of man's history to the end. It opens with God's creation and His eternal plan for His creation. It goes on to tell us how man missed God's purpose; how sin entered the world; and throughout the Old Testament, we see the consequences that sin has brought to man. With the nation of Israel as

---

[1] Even the 'salvation' in Islam (fauz) is different from that of Christianity. In Al-Hilali's Qur'an, it is not even translated as 'salvation', but 'success.' In Islam, it simply means fulfillment of all sensual desires one has always desired on earth.

[2] Suras 5:119; 6:16; 85:11

a case study, the Old Testament shows the plan for man's salvation unraveling until in the New Testament we see God accomplishing man's salvation by sending His Son, Jesus Christ.

When the Lord Jesus came, He demonstrated God's love and salvation by healing the sick, forgiving the sinner, and finally dying for the sinner, rising from the dead, and ascending to heaven to plead for man in the presence of God. The Bible ends with the prediction of the destruction that the entire world will bring on itself and God's ultimate salvation for the redeemed. The entire Bible is on SALVATION and the word appears 180 times in the Bible. But only three times in the whole Qur'an!

Scales of Judgment

The Qur'an says the salvation of man depends on the works he did on earth, and that there will be a scale of judgment in heaven to measure every man's sins.

For example, if you have 50 kilograms of good deeds on one side of the balance and 22 kilograms of wickedness, you will enter paradise.[3] In other words, if one is a murderer, a liar and an adulterer, he can give a lot of alms to the poor to increase the weight on the other side to cancel the evil deeds.

This is a mockery of the seriousness of sin. The Qur'an actually says "good deeds expiate evil deeds." This is not so. If one murders, there is nothing one can do to undo what has been done. An adulterer cannot undo what he has done.

---

3 Sura 7:8; 55:7-9; 101:6-9

Dealing with Sin and the Sinner in Islam

Islam crumbles at the cross. Apart from the deity of Christ, the cross of Christ is the crux of the crisis of Islam. Because Islam does not see the sin question as it really is, it fails to appreciate the purpose of the redemptive work of Jesus Christ. The Qur'an not only rejects the necessity of the crucifixion of Christ, it even tries to deny it historically. By denying the crucifixion of Christ, the Qur'an crucifies itself! It is the cross that shows the awfulness of sin, the seriousness of sin, the wages of sin, the justice of God, the holiness of God and the depth of God's love. No Muslim will repent of his sins unless he understands all these.

The Qur'an quotes the Jewish leaders as boasting that they had killed the Messiah, Jesus the Son of Mary:

> And because of their *(Jews)* saying (in boast), "We killed Messiah 'Isa (Jesus), son of Maryam (Mary), the Messenger of Allah." – but they killed him not, nor crucified him, but the resemblance of 'Isa (Jesus) was put over another man (and they killed that man), and those who differ therein are full of doubts. They have no (certain) knowledge, they follow nothing but conjecture. For surely; they killed him not." [i.e. 'Isa (Jesus), son of Maryam (Mary)].[4]

The Jews could never have made such a statement. They hated Jesus and did not accept Him as their Messiah nor an Apostle of God. That is why they killed Him. They would never have crucified Him if they recognized Him

---

4 Sura 4:157

as the Messiah. That statement is therefore an impossible statement.

This is how the Qur'an crucifies itself in its attempt to deny the crucifixion of Christ. Islam has no answer for the sin question. It can only require physical harm to people, in an attempt to pay for sins:

> "As to the thief, male or female, cut off his or her hands: a punishment by way of example from Allah, for their crime..."[5]

It should not be a surprise that there are many people with missing hands in Islamic nations, or any part of a country where Muslims are in the majority and the Islamic Law, *Sharia*, is in operation. Of course, we do not have sympathy for the thief. However, for a religion that is supposed to bring righteousness, amputation cannot be the solution to the sinfulness of a man. What is the origin of this Qur'anic law of amputation? Ibn Kathir, in his commentary on the Qur'an, says:

> "The cutting of hands as a penalty for theft was practiced by the Arabs in the 'days of paganism', (that is the days known in Islam as 'days of ignorance')."

The Encyclopedia of Islam says this practice was introduced in Arabia by Walib bin Mughirah before Muhammad was born. Mughirah was not a prophet and did not claim any inspiration for such law. Amputation of the thief was already being done in Persia. It was already in the ancient Assyrian Law and the Code of Hammurabi.

---

[5] Sura 5:38

The Assyrian Law says:

> "If a seignior's wife has stolen something from an-other seignior's house, exceeding the value of five minas of lead, the owner of the stolen *(property)* shall swear, 'I never let her take (it); there was a theft in my house;' if the husband so desires, he may give up the stolen and ransom her *(but)* cut off her ears. If her husband does not wish to ran-som her, the owner of the stolen *(property)* shall take her and cut off her nose."[6]

The Code of Hammurabi says when a hired laborer stole the fodder or the seed given to sow, and there was evidence to prove this, the hand should be cut:

> "If a seignior hired a seignior to oversee his field, and lending him feed-grain, entrusting him with oxen, contracted with him to cultivate the field, if that seignior stole the seed or fodder and it has been found in his possession, they shall cut off his hand."[7]

This proves the origin of amputation is pagan, and was practiced 2,000 years before Muhammad was born.

If a thief who stole $200 must face amputation, what would be a fair punishment for a Muslim sheikh, sultan, prince, governor or Head of State who looted the treasury of a province, local government or a whole nation?

---

[6] The Code of Hammurabi, Law 253 in *Ancient Near Eastern Texts Relating to the Old Testament*, ed. James B. Pritchard. Princeton University Press, 1969.
[7] The Code of Hammurabi, Law 253.

We must realize that a sinner always commits more than one sin. For example, an adulterer is also a liar. A thief is also covetous. He is a deceiver and a potential murderer. Yet, even if his hand is cut off, he can still lie and deceive.

Jesus Christ did not come to *punish* sinners. He came to *save* them from their sins and offer them a new life. Amputation may not prevent a thief from stealing.

The Lord Jesus certainly did not view any form of sin with levity. He knew the seriousness of sin; and He warns of the great torment that awaits a sinner in hell fire. In describing the terribleness of hell, He said:

> "And if thy right eye offend thee, pluck it out, and cast it from thee: for it is profitable for thee that one of they members should perish, and not that thy whole body should be cast into hell. And if thy right hand offend thee, cut it off, and cast it from thee: for it is profitable for thee that one of they members should perish, and not that thy whole body should be cast into hell."[8]

It is the *attitude* of hatred for sin that is needed, and not the act itself. That is why Christ's disciples never removed their eyes or cut off their hands. Even when one of them cut off someone's ear, Jesus replaced the ear.[9] With such attitude of dread of hell that the Lord Jesus wanted people to have, He knew that the sin question is far more serious and inherent in man than merely cutting off an arm as a punitive measure as presented in the Qur'an. He

---

8 Matthew 5:29-30
9 Luke 22:50-51

knew that no one would enter heaven with his physical body but with a spiritual body (otherwise there would be blind and lame people in heaven.) Jesus knew sin couldn't be stopped by legislation. In many countries, robbers face execution, yet robbery has increased in such countries. Jesus knew the problem. He said:

> "For from within, out of the heart of men, proceed evil thoughts, adulteries, fornications, murders, thefts, covetousness, wickedness, deceit, lasciviousness, an evil eye, blasphemy, pride, foolishness: All these evil things come from within, and defile the man."[10]

As far as God is concerned, a man does not become a thief only when he steals. As soon as the idea is conceived in his heart, he has become a thief. Many people do not execute their thoughts because they do not have the opportunity or are afraid of being caught. In the sight of God they are no less sinful than those who carry out their plans. A person who does not have a hand, but is a thief in his heart can use his tongue to organize those who do have hands.

So we understand that amputation is NOT a solution to the sin of stealing. God sees stealing and other vices not just as crimes but as sins. If the Qur'an were of divine origin, it would deal with the issue in a more profound way. Amputation does not take away a man's stealing tendency.

The solution God offers in the Bible for any sin is not

---

[10] Mark 7:21-23

to cut off the physical part that a man employs to commit the sin, but rather to give that man a new heart. When the heart, the machinery for the manufacturing of the sins, is changed and the inputs are changed, the products and by-products will change. Not only will the man stop stealing, he will also have a new nature of love that finds expression in giving to others instead of stealing from them. That is why the Apostle Paul wrote to the Ephesian Christians:

> "Let him that stole steal no more: but rather let him labour, working with his hands the thing which is good, that he may have to give to him that needeth."[11]

We should note that the Lord Jesus used the word "thefts," implying that there are various kinds of stealing. For example, gangsters rob a bank, but another kind of stealing can be done by the cashiers at the bank. Still another kind can be done by the bank manager. If the Qur'anic injunction of amputation is God's holy law and therefore cannot be compromised, we wonder how many people will remain in Civil Service and in our corporations.

When Jesus died, He went to paradise with a thief! This thief was the first to benefit from Christ dying for our sins.[12] What happened? This thief did just three things - which every person must do before entering heaven:

1) He knew himself.

2) He knew Jesus.

---

[11] Ephesians 4:28
[12] 1 Corinthians 15:3

3) He repented, calling on Jesus to save him.

The thief knew he was as a sinner who could not save himself, and knew he would soon be in hell fire. Secondly, he recognized the Lord Jesus for who He is. He acknowledged that Jesus is Lord when he cried out for mercy:

"Lord, remember me when thou comest into thy kingdom." [13]

He saw Jesus not just as a fine prophet but also as a Lord who has a Kingdom and who could decide his judgment. The Lord Jesus looked at him and said:

"To day shalt thou be with me in paradise." [14]

And he was.

Judas Iscariot was also a thief. He harbored covetousness in his heart for several years. He heard sermons and deep teachings from the best teacher who ever lived. He had maximum opportunity to repent. Yet because he was known as a religious man and was never caught physically stealing, he thought he was better than those who had no religion. He was an officer of a religion that attracted great multitudes. He became the first Apostle in hell fire!

The lesson here is that you may put on a lot of pretension and sanctimony, harboring covetousness in your heart, stealing with the pen, telling lies to cover fraudulent deals. You may be morally corrupt in your heart, and yet because you are known as very religious, you may silence your conscience and convince yourself that you are not too bad, not as bad as a convicted thief. You may be in

---

[13] Luke 23:42
[14] Luke 23:43

this condition and die with all your hands and legs, but be thrown into hell.

A man can have his hands cut off by the Islamic law. But he will still go to hell if he does not receive Jesus. If a man will enter heaven, it will not be because he didn't have a hand to steal with. It will be because he trusted Christ for salvation. Then he will personally hate that sin because of God's Holy Spirit within him.

We have searched the Qur'an for a definite plan of salvation of man from sin, its power and its consequence, but we have found none. ***No Muslim can be sure of his salvation.***

> "... nor do I know what will be done with me or with you (my followers)..." said Muhammad himself.[15]

Unfortunately, when leaders of Islam are confronted with these issues by an honest Muslim seeker, the ready-made answer is: "the author has blasphemed, and we must deal with him." But that is not an answer. When some people have no answer for certain ultimate questions, it often leads to violence. Such attitude is folly. Nobody knows everything. We must be humble enough to learn more.

---

15 Sura 46:9

10

Test of Authenticity

In an attempt to secure people's confidence in the authenticity of his revelations, the speaker in the Qur'an is heard swearing by pen, record, signs of the zodiac, the sun, the moon, etc.,[1] How is this linked with the common superstitions of pagan Arabians? What link has that with idolatry?

Some Muslims say there is no link. We understand that because of their love for their religion. We need sincerity with ourselves if we really desire the truth. We all agree that when a man swears, he does so by a power higher than himself. Islam teaches that there is no deity other than Allah, and that even the idols of Meccans, including Allat, al-Manat and al-Uzzah were mere fictitious names given by men, and that there are no powers or beings behind those idols. Sura 69:38-47 says:

---

[1] Suras 44:2; 53:1-5; 68:1; 90:1; 91:1, etc.

"I swear by all that you can see, and all that is hidden from your view, that this *(recitation of the Qur'an)* is the utterance of a noble messenger... It is no soothsayer's divination; how little you reflect! It is a revelation of the Lord of the universe. Had he *(Muhammad)* invented lies about Us *(Allah)*, we would have seized him by the right hand and severed his heart's vein: not one of you could have protected him"[2]

"I swear by all that you can see..." What does this mean? We believe it means "I swear by all the physical objects around you here."

First, we know that when a man swears by God, he is calling upon "God" as a witness. When one swears by a physical image, it is the being behind that image that one is invoking to bear witness to one's words.

In Sura 90:1, we read, "I swear by this town (Mecca)." In Sura 2-91:1, he swore by the sun and the moon. Our Muslim friends say it is Allah, not Muhammad speaking in the Qur'an. Is Allah then swearing?

If Muhammad swears by *Qalam* (pen), is the pen an idol? The Muslim may say no, but what is an idol? It is a physical or mental image to which a man attaches importance or ascribes power. The image is believed to have powers behind it, which come from living spiritual beings.

The power behind an idol is always greater than its patron. Swearing is done in its name because the worshipper

---

[2] Daood's translation

believes that he is bound by the power of the idol, and that the idol is capable of harming him if he swears falsely.

In the Qur'an, Muhammad swears by Allah. But he also swears by other things. That means he accorded power and deity to these other beings. That destroys the basic Islamic confession "There is no god beside Allah..."

Moreover, if Muhammad was a prophet, a spokesman of the Almighty God, why did he have to swear to convince his people of the divine origin of his words?

Since a man has to swear by a power higher than himself or at least by himself,[3] why was the swearing done by *Qalam* (pen), *Dhuha* (the rising sun), the moon, the signs of the Zodiac and the city of Mecca?

If Allah is speaking, then he is the one swearing. If Allah swears (that is, binds himself by oaths to other powers), does he remain the almighty as Muslims claim? Jesus Christ taught His disciples:

> "But I say unto you, Swear not at all; neither by heaven; for it is God's throne: Nor by the earth; for it is his footstool: neither by Jerusalem; for it is the city of the great King... But let your communication be, Yea, yea; Nay, nay: for whatsoever is more than these cometh of evil." [4]

The Lord Jesus received much opposition, especially from religious people; but He never swore in an attempt to prove anything. He said:

> "If I do not do the works of My Father, believe me

---

[3] See Hebrews 6:13 and 16.
[4] Matthew 5:34-37

not. But if I do, though ye believe not me, believe the works: that ye may know, and believe, that the Father is in me, and I in him."[5]

Jesus Christ proved and validated His claims of Lordship by demonstrating His power over nature.

The early Christians, too, did not have to swear to prove they were speaking the very words of God as taught by Christ. The evidence was readily available and could not be denied by their enemies.[6] The writer of Hebrews also says:

> "For if the word spoken by angels was steadfast, and every transgression and disobedience received a just recompence of reward; How shall we escape, if we neglect so great salvation; which at the first began to be spoken by the Lord, and was confirmed unto us by them that heard him; God also bearing them witness, both with signs and wonders, and with divers miracles, and gifts of the Holy Ghost, according to his own will?"[7]

They received the Word of the Lord directly from the disciples of Christ who were with Him and heard Him speak. The Lord Himself confirmed their words, "bearing them witness, both with signs and wonders, and with divers miracles, and gifts of the Holy Ghost" that followed. No need of swearing.

That is also why Jesus and His disciples did not have

---

[5] John 10:37-38
[6] See Acts 4:13-16
[7] Hebrews 2:2-4

to fight any Jihad (Holy War) to spread their faith. The Apostle James wrote:

> "But above all things, my brethren, swear not, neither by heaven, neither by the earth, neither by any other oath: but let your yea be yea; and your nay, nay; lest ye fall into condemnation."[8]

---

[8] James 5:12

11

Biblical Blunders in the Qur'an

The Islamic Bibliophobia

As we pointed out earlier, Muhammad said he came, not to bring any "new-fangled doctrine,"[1] but to confirm the books of the Bible. A person who has not properly compared the Qur'an with the Bible may accept such a claim. But there is not one accurate Biblical story in the entire Qur'an. There is virtually no complete Bible story in any sura. Many stories begin at the middle and end before the their real conclusion.

Islamic leaders today realize that if they allow their followers to read the Bible, they will discover the truth and most likely prefer the stories and testimonies of the Bible. Muslims will discover that the Qur'an did not come to "confirm" the Bible as it claims.

---

[1] Sura 46:9

This is why Islamic nations see the distribution of the Bible as dangerous. They are so afraid of this book! Even with their slogan "The Bible has been corrupted," they will not allow their people to see the "corruption" from the book directly so they can decide for themselves. They would rather attack the Bible from a distance.

In September 1992, a Saudi Arabian citizen, Sidiq Mulallah, was beheaded by the Saudi government. His offenses:

1) He, a Muslim, abandoned Islam and embraced Christianity, a sin punishable by death, according to the Qur'an:

> "...But if they turn back (from Islam), take (hold of) them and kill them wherever you find them..."[2]

2) He, Sidiq, brought a copy of the Bible into Saudi Arabia, Allah's sacred land.[3]

Islamic leaders have good reasons to fear the Bible. The Qur'an states in many places that it came to "confirm" the Christian and the Jewish scriptures. But Muslim leaders have discovered that such claims will suffer if they allow their followers to learn the truth for themselves.

In this last chapter, we will carefully examine the Qur'an to learn whether or not it really came to confirm the Bible.

---

[2] Sura 4:89
[3] News Network International, January 1, 1993. Taken from the U.S. State Department Human Rights Report.

Fallacies

There is scarcely any biblical character mentioned in the Qur'an that is not historically "assassinated." There are many evil deeds and sins the Qur'an falsely attributes to these holy men of God.

Abraham: All Muslims believe Abraham to be a Muslim and hold him in high esteem. He is to them an epitome of righteousness and faith. But the character and the whole history of Abraham are ghastly wounded. According to the Bible, there were two occasions where Abraham lied in order to protect his life from the covetousness of the Pharaoh of Egypt and Abimelech of Gerar. He said Sarah was his sister. Of course, this was not a complete lie because Sarah was his half-sister.[4] Apart from this act, the Bible nowhere ascribes any sin to Abraham.

In the Qur'an, even though Sura 3:67 says Abraham did not join partners with God, he is accused of idolatry in another sura. He is presented as worshipping the star, then the moon, and then the sun, calling each "My Lord."[5] If Abraham ever did adore the star, the moon, and the sun, saying to each, "This is my Lord," he also must have been guilty of adding partners to God.

The Qur'an does not tell us that Abraham repented of this sin of sun-moon adoration and attributing lordship to them. But even if he repented, this was already an *unforgivable sin* according to Muhammad's own definition of *shirk*. Since Abraham is not seen repenting of such an act, and the Qur'an regards Abraham as a perfect example

---

[4] Genesis 12:10-20; 20:1-18
[5] Sura 6:75-78

of a Muslim, does that not mean that in Islam, regarding the moon or the sun as "My Lord," is not un-Islamic?

Of the sun, he said, "This is the greatest (of all of his other Lords)" or "This is the greater (of any other Lord)" in some other translations (verse 78). This destroys the Islamic confession *"Allahu Akbar"* (Allah is the greater).

There are no righteous people in the Bible that worshipped the moon, the star, or the sun. They all regarded such an act as great infidelity. The patriarch Job said:

> "If I beheld the sun when it shined, or the moon walking in brightness; And my heart hath been secretly enticed, or my mouth hath kissed my hand (in adoration): This also were an iniquity to be punished by the judge: for I should have denied the God that is above."[6]

Apart from Jesus Christ, there is no biblical character in the Qur'an that the book does not record a sin for. Many Islamic publications argue that since the Bible records the sins of the prophets of God, it could not be the Word of God. We find that the Qur'an records not only the sins of the prophets, *but even sins they never committed!*

Worship of the moon and other heavenly bodies was a major idolatrous practice at the time Islam emerged. Muhammad condemned idolatry, especially the worship of the physical images in the Ka'aba shrine. But we have never seen where he condemned the worship of the moon, which was the greatest form of idolatry in Arabia. If he did not believe in it, why would he say that Abraham

---

[6] Job 31:26-28

(supposedly the father of Islam) also worshipped the moon? Was Muhammad, the author of the Qur'an, justifying moon worship?

The modern American or European Muslim may say no. Then we may ask: what link has the symbol of the crescent moon and the star on the minaret of every mosque? Why is the moon seen as a major Islamic symbol on the flags of Islamic nations and on most Islamic decorations? Apart from the purpose of a lunar month calculation, what links have the moon and the rising sun with the Ramadan fast and Islamic festivals? Why did Muhammad swear by the crescent moon and the star?

Facing East To Pray

There are two reasons why Muhammad commanded Muslims to face the east while praying. From Medina, where he gave the order, Mecca is to the east. Facing east therefore means facing the Black Stone in Mecca, and facing the direction of *Dhuha*, the rising sun. A Muslim who does not want to face the truth may deny this, but this was already common among the idolaters of the Middle East and dates back before Muhammad. Facing the east has always meant worshipping the heavenly bodies[7] and God dealt with Israel severely when she started copying the nations surrounding her in this practice.

Historio-Linguistic Errors

The Bible says the name of Abraham's father was Terah. The Qur'an says Azar (Azir in some translations);.[8] Some

---

[7] Ezekiel 8:16; Isaiah 2:5-6
[8] Sura 6:74

Muslim commentators and translators put Terah in brackets wherever Azar is mentioned, hoping to make us believe the two words are the same. This is an unsuccessful and unacceptable reconciliation attempt. The two words have no historio-linguistic link.

How many children did Abraham have? The Qur'an says two. The Bible records eight.[9]

Contrary to the Qur'an, there is no record that Abraham ever lived in Mecca or worshipped in any Ka'aba shrine. He lived in Hebron in Israel, where he died and where his grave remains today. His hometown was Ur of the Chaldeans, not Mecca. This is the history, and we must separate history from religious myths.

Noah

How many children did Noah have? The Qur'an says one son, and he drowned in the flood. So by implication, only Noah (and his wife, though not indicated) survived the flood.[10] In truth, Noah had three sons and none drowned in the flood. All three entered the Ark with their wives.[11] The Qur'an even says Noah's wife and Lot's wife perished "in the fire."[12] Which fire? Did Noah and Lot's wife live at the same time? Moreover, if the only son of Noah perished in the flood, and his wife perished in a fire, how then was the earth populated after the Flood?

All Muslims had believed that the flood in the time of Noah was universal. Now that Christians are pointing out

---

[9] Genesis 25:1-6, 9
[10] Sura 11:42-43
[11] Genesis 6-7
[12] Sura 66:10

the errors in the flood story of the Qur'an, some Muslims (who believe it is their duty to defend the Qur'an at any cost) want to reject the universality of the deluge so the Qur'an would not be faulted.

This is a cheap way of escape. Some geologists who say the flood was local are evolutionists, and no Muslim can believe in the theory of evolution and still believe in the Qur'an. If the flood was a local phenomenon, God would have asked Noah and his family to flee to another location rather than asking him to build such a massive ark that took him several years to build. The birds could have flown and migrated to another area for a season.

Of Moses and Aaron

Who adopted Moses? The Qur'an says Pharaoh's wife.[13] In the Bible, Moses himself wrote it was Pharaoh's daughter.[14]

Where was Moses' first encounter with God? The Qur'an says, the Valley of Tuwa.[15] The Bible says Mount Horeb.[16]

The episode of the apostasy of the children of Israel in which they made a golden calf to worship is grossly distorted in the Qur'an. This story is recorded in not less than three places in the Qur'an, each of which is different from the others. Either Muhammad got his stories from different sources or he only overheard them on different occasions and recited each as he "received" it. After his

---

[13] Sura 28:9
[14] Exodus 2:5-10
[15] Suras 20:12 and 79:16
[16] Exodus 3:1-6

death, his devotees possibly did not notice any discrepancies; they just gathered all they could and compiled them as "the Holy Qur'an." We read from the Qur'an:

> "(Allah) said: Verily, We have tried thy people in thy absence: The Samaris has led them astray."[17]

Allah says he tried the people (Israel) when Moses was not around. What was the trial? It was Israel making an idol to worship. This raises a serious moral question that is prevalent in the character of Allah, his tempting people to sin.[18] Here the Qur'an says Allah tempted Israel to worship a golden calf as God Almighty. In the Bible account, it was God who called Moses to "come up hither" to the mount, very near where the people were, to give him all the laws and commandments:

> "And the LORD said unto Moses, Come up to me into the mount, and be there: and I will give thee tables of stone, and a law, and commandments which I have written; that thou mayest teach them. And Moses rose up, and his minister Joshua: and Moses went up into the mount of God. And he said unto the elders, Tarry ye here for us, until we come again unto you: and, behold, Aaron and Hur are with you: if any man have any matters to do, let him come unto them. And Moses went up into the mount, and a cloud covered the mount. ...and Moses was in the mount forty days and forty nights."[19]

---

[17] See Sura 20:85-96.

[18] Sura 14:4

[19] Exodus 24:12-15, 18

If it was Allah who tried Israel in Moses' absence, how would he gain in so doing? The second point is the statement, "The Samaris has misled them into error." Other translations say "As Samiri" (the Samaritan) and "Samari."[20] The first statement says Allah tempted them into the error. The second statement says "the Samaritan" or "As Samari" tried them. Maybe that is not a serious contradiction. Maybe it means Allah stirred up "the Samaritan" to do the misleading. This is not strange because many verses in the Qur'an say Allah misleads people into sin.[21]

A fundamental issue raised in this verse is the presence of the word "Samaritan." If a Muslim knew history, he would question the heavenly origin of the Qur'an at this point. When the Qur'an was written, Arabs did not know much history since most of them were illiterate, including Muhammad (according to the claim of Muslims). The city of Samaria did not exist at the time Moses was leading the children of Israel. It was built hundreds of years after Israel settled in the Promised Land. Therefore, saying a Samaritan led Israel into error in the wilderness is a serious historical fallacy.

Secondly, the original writer of the Qur'an did not know the geography of this area. At the time of the episode in question, the children of Israel were in Sinai. An old Arabic Christian apologetic, *Al-Hidaya (The True Guidance)* says:

> "The mention of the Samaritan indicates substantial ignorance of history and geography. We

---

[20] Sura 20:87, 95-96
[21] See for instance Suras 16:93; 42:44 and 74:31.

do not know how or from where this Samaritan came. Did he descend from heaven or rise from below?" [22]

Perhaps the calf made in the wilderness is being confused with the two gold calves Jeroboam made for Israel in Bethel and Dan in his new kingdom, which later had Samaria as its capital. If that is the source of the error, how can we say the Qur'an came from heaven or was inspired by an all-knowing God? This is an honest question we have to answer. Religious sentiment won't help us. We must choose between history and myths.

From real history, the biblical account, it was not "the thing," the calf, that tempted the children of Israel. Neither was it any Samaritan (who didn't exist then) or "As Samaris." Neither was it God who tried them. It was Aaron who made the calf for them because he feared the threat of the people.

If the Qur'an were written in heaven, or inspired by the true God, how could these obvious ridiculous historical blunders find their way there? From the foregoing, it would be wrong to claim that the Bible and the Qur'an are ALMOST the same thing. They are not.

Jesus Christ

Since Islam does not allow independent thinking, Muslim leaders scare their followers from the Bible, so Muslims do not know what they are missing by not reading the gospel accounts of Jesus Christ. A Muslim who

---

[22] *The True Guidance* (Villach: Light of Life, P.O. Box 13, A9503, Austria.

ignores the slogan that "the Bible has been corrupted" and studies it will know within himself that what he is reading is the true account of the life and words of Jesus Christ, as opposed to the confusions of the Qur'an.

The "Jesus" of the Qur'an has no cross. He never died and therefore did not resurrect. While there are over 43 beautiful illustrative parables in the gospel accounts, the Jesus of the Qur'an spoke not one parable. The beautiful Sermon on the Mount is absent in the Qur'an. He had no verbal confrontation with the Pharisees, Sadducees or Scribes. His disciples are not mentioned. The Qur'an only speaks of His friends. There is no definite teaching of Christ. There is no description of any of Christ's miracles (while 38 miracles are recorded in the gospel accounts, plus several non-detailed healings of multitudes). The biblical "miracles" described in the Qur'an are confused, while others are taken directly from a book of fables.

The Qur'anic Jesus is a Jesus who receives a query in heaven for allowing people to worship him as God. We see this Jesus trembling before God, denying a claim of deity.[23] Such a Jesus is simply not the Jesus Christ of history. He is a personal imagination.

However, the Jesus in the Qur'an is still born of the Virgin Mary, is blessed by God[24] and is strengthened by the Holy Spirit.[25] He is the Word of God, knowing the unknown. He spoke in the cradle (a story taken from

---

[23] Sura 5:116
[24] Sura 43:61, 63; 19:30
[25] Sura 2:253

a book of fables).[26] He healed the lepers and raised the dead, and created a bird.[27]

A sincere Muslim will realize that even in the Qur'an Jesus is more than a prophet. He is mentioned 97 times, to Muhammad's 25. Jesus is the only sinless man in the Qur'an (Sura 19:19). Adam sinned (Sura 2:36; 7:22-23). Abraham sinned (Sura 26:82). Moses sinned (Sura 28:15-16). Jonah sinned (Sura 37:142). David sinned (Sura 38:24-25). Muhammad constantly asks for forgiveness of his own personal sins.[28] All prophets sinned. Indeed…

> "For all have sinned, and come short of the glory of God;"[29]

No Muslim can know the real Jesus unless he studies the Bible. From the Bible you will see clearly a thirty-year-old man who, in three years of ministry, changed the course of man's history forever.

How could the Qur'an be the "fuller explanation" of the gospel of Jesus Christ when in it, all the major aspects of Christ's life and teaching are missing, and the stories of other chief biblical characters like David, Solomon and Noah are all grossly distorted and confused?

The editor of the Hadith says:

> "The Qur'an is the greatest wonder among the wonders of the world. It repeatedly challenged the people of the world to bring a chapter like it, but

---

26 Sura 3:46; 5:110
27 Suras 3:49; 5:110
28 Sura 33:36-38; 47:19; 48:1-2
29 Romans 3:23

they failed and the challenge remains unanswered up to this day..."[30]

The Qur'an could indeed be a wonder to the 7th century Arabs because of the illiteracy of the people of Arabia at the time. Today, they are learned, but they are not allowed to challenge the Qur'an. Any Muslim who dares to challenge a claim in the Qur'an is regarded as an infidel and a blasphemer, and faces a threat. Some Muslims have questions they want to ask but they must not voice their suspicions—even when they see an obvious scientific blunder!

For example, what does a modern Muslim do with Sura 18:85-98 (*Kahf*)? This passage gives a narrative about Alexander the Great and his exploits, and ends with a statement concerning the setting of the sun, and therefore the shape of the planet Earth.

Primitive Arabs, like most people in their time, wondered where the sun went in the evening, and how it came up again in the morning. Here is the answer from a book supposedly given by the creator of the sun and the earth.

> "He (i.e. Zul-qarnaim) followed, until he reaching the setting of the sun. He found it set in a spring of murky water."[31]

Islamic scholars all agree that Zul-qarnaim is Alexander the Great. Yusuf Ali agrees with this in his translation of the Qur'an. The passage here says that Alexander took, as part of his world conquest, a journey westward to reach

---

[30] Mishkat'ul Masabih, Vol. 3, p. 664.
[31] Sura 18:85-86

the end of the world. He followed the sun until he found out that the end of the world was where the sun went down—under the murky waters of a pond. As the sun was submerged under the murky water, darkness came upon the earth.

To the primitive Arabs, this was a fantastic revelation from Allah, the all-knowing, and it was a proof of Muhammad's prophet-hood.

The problem here is that the writer of the Qur'an thought the sun was as small at it looks to the eyes of man on earth, and so it could enter a muddy pond. Moreover, the writer thought that a man could follow the sun in a linear direction. This is from the primitive belief that the earth is flat. The writer did not know that the earth is spherical and revolves around the sun.

Such a mistake is pardonable for primitive Arabs, and for Muhammad because of his education and exposure. But how can a modern Muslim still claim that this is a revelation from Allah and one of the proofs of the divine origin of the Qur'an?

Someone may say, "I see your point, but I don't care. Even if there is a scientific error in the Qur'an, I still believe it came from God." Of course you have the right to remain ignorant. But as Dr. Robert Morey said, when arrogance is added to ignorance, it leads to fanaticism.

In a way, the Qur'an is a wonder, even today; but the wonder is the claim of its heavenly origin. Those who are well-informed wonder how it could have originated from God. The German author, Salomon Reinach, said:

"It is humiliating to the human intellect to think
that this mediocre literature has been the subject
of innumerable commentaries and that millions
of men are still wasting time in absorbing it."[32]

The writer of the Qur'an challenged his illiterate audience to write a chapter like any in the Qur'an. Some of
us are amused by such a challenge. Why should anyone
want to write a book like this, a book with neither serious research nor any respect for historical and scientific
facts?

However the challenge to "bring a chapter like it" has
been challenged. The problem is that Islamic leaders do
not like "the people of the world" (non-Muslims) to analyze the Qur'an. Those who challenged the authenticity of
the Qur'an were seen by Muhammad as great enemies of
Islam, and they faced the wrath of Muslims.

One example was Abdollah Sarh, a learned man and a
close associate of Muhammad. He was said to have been
involved in the composition of the Qur'an, and he always
suggested areas to be amended before public presentation
by Muhammad.

After some time, however, Sarh felt he could not con-
tinue deceiving himself. He left Islam and joined the
Quraysh people, the chief opponents of Muhammad.
Because Sarh knew some secrets about the "heavenly
descent" of the Qur'an, he was very dangerous to Islam.
When Muhammad conquered Mecca, Sarh was silenced

[32] Reinach, Salomon, *Orpheus: A History of Religion* (New York:
Livercraft, Inc., 1932) p. 176.

by the edge of the sword. He was one of the very first people killed.[33]

The challenge does not remain "unanswered up to this day." Many books expose the problems of the Qur'an. One example is *The Islamic Invasion* by Dr. Robert Morey.[34] A number of Muslims have read this excellent book in the United States and have abandoned Islam. Islamic leaders try to suppress such publications because they are greatly afraid of such answers from non-Muslims.

This book is another attempt to answer the challenges of Islamic books that exalt the Qur'an and attack the Bible. The attitude of Muslim leaders to this will be more proof of how intolerant they are to challenges of the Qur'an. This book is only a summary of the problems of the Qur'an. A thorough comparison of the Qur'an, the Bible and secular history would take several volumes.

Many of these errors in the Qur'an—historical fallacies and anachronisms, plagiarism of fables and folktales, incomplete stories, endless repetitions, illogicality, disjointed and convoluted grammar and syntax, trivialities and myriads of contradictions—would have been pardonable as an evidence of a human hand who was unlettered. They would have been overlooked if Muslims had not claimed that the Qur'an was the Word of God dictated to Muhammad piece by piece or given to him as a book

---

[33] Ali, *23 Years: A Study of the Prophetic Career of Mouhammad*, p 98. See also the *Sunan abu-Dawud*, Book 14, #2677 and Book 38, #4345-4346.
[34] Morey, Robert, *The Islamic Invasion*, (Eugene: Harvest House Publishers, 1992). Also see *Christ, Muhammad and I* by Mohammad Al Ghazoli (2007). Both are available from Chick Publications.

once preserved on a tablet in heaven, which had not been changed in any way. If they had not claimed that the book is devoid of errors or if they had not said the Qur'an is a miracle, nay, the greatest and "the ultimate miracle" in the literary world; if they had not taunted the Bible, scholars might have pardoned these massive mistakes..

For decades, many Muslim commentators have sweated profusely in unsuccessful attempts to explain away these charges. But the issues involved here take more than noise and slogans to dismiss. Until they succeed, it is only reasonable and rational to dismiss the claim of the heavenly authorship of the Qur'an as grotesque, wicked and monstrous. It is wicked because the claim has led at least a billion souls into a Christless eternity. It has put countless millions in spiritual and intellectual bondage. But the bold among them can free themselves from this bondage.

What the Qur'an Does NOT Say

The Qur'an does NOT say that:

- Muhammad is the savior of anybody.

- A Muslim can be 100% sure of his own salvation.

- The Qur'an was never changed.

- A Muslim should not study the Bible.

- The Qur'an is a substitute for an original lost Bible.

- The Qur'an has no error.

Therefore, if a Muslim refuses to study the Bible, it is not because the Qur'an says he should not. It is because his Imams and self acclaimed "Islamic scholars" do not want such a Muslim to be exposed to the truth.

Finally, if you are a Muslim, consider this: If God takes your soul tonight and you find yourself in hell, who is to blame? If you despise knowledge and ignore His wisdom (for fear of other Muslims or because there are some rich and learned people in Islam), God says He will laugh at you when your destruction comes:

> "Because I have called, and ye refused; I have stretched out my hand, and no man regarded; But ye have set at nought all my counsel, and would (take) none of my reproof:

> "I also will laugh at your calamity; I will mock when your fear cometh; When your fear cometh as desolation, and your destruction cometh as a whirlwind; when distress and anguish cometh upon you. Then shall they call upon me, but I will not answer; they shall seek me early, but they shall not find me;

> "For that they hated knowledge, and did not choose the fear of the LORD: They would none of my counsel: they despised all my reproof. Therefore shall they eat of the fruit of their own way, and be filled with their own devices. For the turning away of the simple shall slay them, and the prosperity of fools shall destroy them. But whoso hearkeneth unto me shall dwell safely, and shall be quiet from fear of evil."[35]

Yes, the blame will be yours for ignoring your opportunity for salvation.

---

[35] Proverbs 1:24-33

BUT YOU DON'T HAVE TO PERISH!

Here is a letter I received from a Muslim...

"I FOUND JESUS"

"An evangelist... gave me a copy of your book, 'Anatomy of the Qur'an'.[36] It was as if everything I had held dear from childhood crumbled. I was brought up in a strict Islamic education right from the elementary Arabic/Qur'anic school. My father is a popular Imam in this area. After my first reading of the book, I went to my father to ask him some questions on Islam and our prophet. Instead of answering the questions, he suspected I had been reading some dangerous Christian books and warned me sternly. He found out the book, burnt it, and collected the ashes to make some charms.

"I got another copy because there were still a number of things I wanted to verify. At a point in reading I got confused.

"From the facts in the book, I had no much problem making up my mind concerning Al-Qur'an. But how could Jesus be what Christians say he is? That was my real problem. How could he be 'the Way'? Suddenly I fell into a dream-like state. I saw a human figure, but not flesh; it was a transparent light. The figure said in a very loud voice. 'I

---

[36] 1st Edition, 1994.

am the One!' The voice was so loud that I had to cover my ears.

"As I opened my eyes, my hands were still on my ears. I felt the presence of God in that room so powerfully I began to weep. I was convinced the Lord has appeared to me in love. My confusion vanished. When I told my father, he went to call an Islamic priest more powerful than himself, and they prepared and gave me some Qur'anic concoction to drink, to turn my mind back to 'normal.'

"From that day, I knew I could not continue in Islam again. I started going to Deeper Life Bible Church fellowship secretly - until the bubble burst! My father discovered when a brother from the Church came visiting. I wasn't around. He met my father and asked for 'Brother Kamar.' I almost lost my life in the struggle and persecution that followed this.

"But the more hated I was, the more convinced I became about what I have read in your book."

— Kamar, M.

What will your decision be? I suggest that you believe everything the Bible says about you:

a) You are a sinner and your righteousness cannot save you.

b) No sinner will enter heaven if he dies in his sins.

c) Believe all that the Bible says about Jesus Christ: that

God sent Him to die for your sin—that He is the Son of the living God who says:

> "I am the way, the truth, and the life: no man cometh unto the Father, but by me."[37]

d) Confess your sin of unbelief and pride, and invite Jesus Christ into your heart to be your Lord and Saviour.

e) Get a Bible and study it daily. Start with the New Testament.

f) Reject and renounce the spirits of any religion. Only the Bible offers you the definite and sure way of salvation.

g) Ask the Holy Spirit to take control of your life.

h) Pray daily, and thank God for hearing your prayers.

i) Ask God to lead you to a Bible-believing church. Introduce yourself to the pastor and tell him you want to be baptized.

If you have just taken a bold step of faith to come to Christ, and you want to be remembered in our prayers on specific issues, email us at:

shalom.moshay@gmail.com.

---

[37] John 14:6